Independent's Guide to Overthrowing the Two-Party System

by James R Duncan

www.primallightpress.com

Primal Light Press

www.primallightpress.com

Library of Congress Cataloging-in-Publication Data

ISBN Number 978-0-9976302-2-0

Book Cover Design and Interior Illustrations by KD Solutions
www.knoitalldesigns.com

Printed in the United States of America

"We have it in our power to begin the world over again…"

—Thomas Paine

Introduction

Let's Fix Things... Now

America is going crazy, right? We've got online ranting and riots, threats of impeachment, cops killing people, and people killing cops. There have been investigations into corrupted elections, the longest government shutdown in history, Supreme Court nominees accused of sexual assault, and those all-too-frequent mass shootings. And the mainstream media makes way more money off fanning the partisan flames than they do in trying to give you unbiased reporting, with American polarization and chaos getting more intense every day. This isn't the way it's supposed to be, is it?

You probably want to do something to help, to change things for the better, but who's got the time to wade through complex political muck to figure out who's right and wrong? Where can you turn?

Answer: **this book**

(And you're in luck, you don't even have to read it all!)

What This Book Is NOT...

- Despite its catchy title and cover, this book is NOT advocating rebellion against the US government, nor even dismantling the Republican or Democratic parties.

- This book is NOT an attempt to establish any specific new political parties, nor side with any version of the currently existing right, left, Libertarians, Socialists, Greens, NRA, Tea Party, Black Lives Matter, Blue Lives Matter, Communists, or any other existing organization or pre-labeled ideology.

- And, it is NOT advocating violence of any kind...

What This Book Is...

- A comprehensive resource to help politically independent thinkers find good ideas from the right, left, or anywhere else, while avoiding groupthink, political-party bullshit.

- An easy-to-understand strategic framework for you, the American individual, to permanently increase your own political power by lessening entrenched two-party (Republicans and Democrats') control.

- A guidebook, for all who can't buy into Republican and Democratic propaganda anymore, to fix our broken political system, eliminate corruption, and lessen the red-versus-blue divisions across our country.

Simply put, this book intends to empower you, whoever you are and whatever your views, over corrupted politicians, lobbyists, and a governmental system that has become woefully dysfunctional. It is designed to be an evolving one-stop resource for political independents to understand issues and take actions. This book does not claim to be intellectually perfect, or even currently complete, but only a much needed starting point.

In fact, we highly encourage you to go to **independ.me** to lend your voice to creating a vibrant movement of political independents. The book is projected to be updated with election cycles in order to get even more relevant and timely on what actions can best help empower political independence. You can help shape its direction through making suggestions at **independ.me** for any groups, discussions, and ideas you think should be supported or dropped from future editions. Even criticism is great, so that we can double-check our own thinking and correct any missteps. You can also go to the "Independ Me" youtube channel and subscribe.

With your help, we can hopefully move to a multiparty system, or at least become unchained from the forced false choice between only two bad political options. The goal of this book is to help America's system become more democratic, functional, and thereby lessen the angry polarization the two major political parties, and their media wings, are intentionally exacerbating.

And there's no wrong way for you to get involved. Just skip to whatever section grabs your interest and start there. If you've got the ebook version links are provided, while if you've got the print version you will have to google suggested resources. The important thing is to start doing something now and to spread the ideas in this book that make sense to you.

Improvement begins as the two-party system ends! All it takes is for you to be sick of elephants and donkeys alike, and to stop participating in that false binary choice of red versus blue. So let's do this, fellow American, let's save our democracy...

Table of Contents

Part One

The Problem

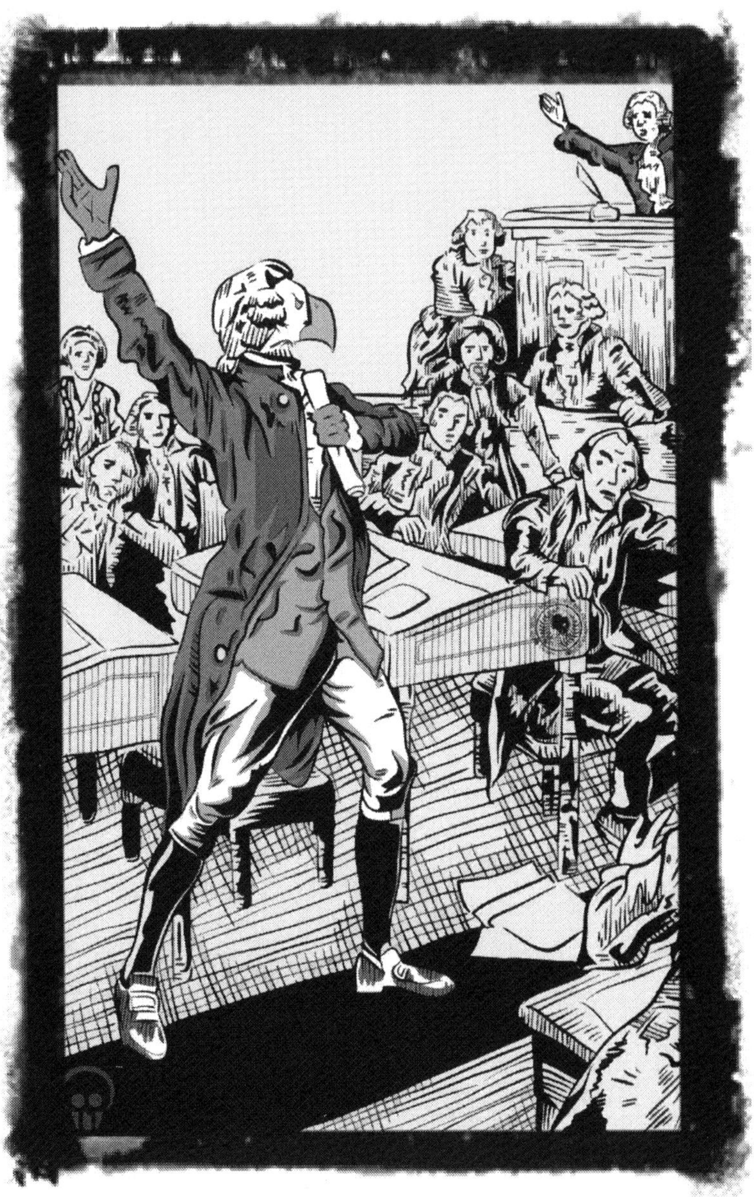

"Give me liberty, or give me death!"

—Patrick Henry

Chapter One
America Is Broken
(Or, at least, it can be improved)

On June 14, 2017, a Democrat attacked Republican Congressional members at a baseball practice in Washington, DC. It was a bloody act of domestic political terrorism that briefly shocked America, often now numb to gun violence, into musings of a possible second civil war.

After the event, commentator Peggy Noonan wrote in the *Wall Street Journal*: "What we are living through in America is not only a division but a great estrangement. It is between those who support Donald Trump and those who despise him, between left and right, between the two parties, and even to some degree between the bases of those parties and their leaders in Washington. It is between the religious and those who laugh at Your Make Believe Friend, between cultural progressives and those who wish not to have progressive ways imposed upon them...We look down on each other, fear each other, increasingly hate each other."

This rise of American political hate between right and left can no longer be denied. In its largest-ever poll, *Political Polarization in the American Public*, Pew Research confirmed this extremism is at an all-time high. In October 2018 the country even saw shocking new political terrorism with sixteen bombs being mailed to various critics of President Trump, including former Democratic presidents and candidates. What lies ahead? It seems more and more Americans blindly support a red or blue banner so extremely that they will resort to hate, arguing, and even violence, while the rest of us now only want to disengage to avoid all the ugliness. Something has gone wrong in this country, and it needs to be fixed.

It is the proposition of this book that political hate

among Americans has risen in lockstep with the political class of Republican and Democratic oligarchs becoming more corrupt and entrenched, while the "American Dream" continues to evaporate for most everyone else. The problem is not either only the Republicans or the Democrats, but the entirety of our two-party system itself. And to clarify, this is not to say that every single Republican or Democrat is bad, or every one of their ideas wrong, but that the two-party system has morphed into its own out-of-control illness sickening the country. Basically, most Republican and Democratic leaders are doing a shitty job of everything except getting themselves and their 1 percent friends rich. Yet, because of your perpetually increasing frustration with your own American life, you keep buying their blue vs. red propaganda and turning on your neighbor instead of them. This isn't crazed conspiracy, it's just the predictable outcome of the system we currently have set up.

For examples of its systemic dysfunction, consider:

- Since the 1970s, Inequality.org reports that median income growth for all American citizens has consistently slowed, while the wealth gap between the upper 1 percent and 99 percent of the country has consistently widened. The rich keep getting richer and everyone else slips further behind.

- For the first time in almost a hundred years, American life expectancy has fallen for three consecutive years, including perpetually rising suicide rates and the highest drug-related deaths in its history. This is despite having the most expensively burdensome health care system in the world, according to *The Washington Post*

- *The Guardian* has reported that Since 1968 there

have been more gun deaths of American citizens on US soil (1,516,863) than there have been American citizens killed in all our wars (1,396,733), despite America having the highest incarnation rate of its own citizens in the world through a multi-billion-dollar private-prison industry.

- A 2018 United Way study found almost half of all Americans are struggling to pay for shelter and food, despite our country having low unemployment, historic stock market gains, and exponential increases in technological innovation.

- According to the Peter G Petersen Foundation's review of the Congressional Budget Office's report, while polls on Americans' satisfaction with how government operates have consistently lowered over the past 20 years, government spending and debt has consistently risen (projected to be 108 percent of GDP in 2020). Always spending more, with always worse results.

- In 2016, for the first time ever, the well-respected *Economist* magazine dropped America out of its highest tier "full democracy" category and into a "flawed democracy" rank alongside many third-world countries with systemic privacy, due-process, corruption, and civil-rights concerns.

Obviously, depending on your own biases (we all have them), the relevance of these listed facts is debatable. Suffice to say, however, most Americans don't currently think things are going as well as they could be.

Maybe you see big government as the problem, or maybe you believe society needs more regulation to ensure everyone is treated fairly. Maybe you believe the "bad people" in society causing the problems are blacks or whites, males or females, liberals or conservatives, church-goers or scientists, a corrupt president or a corrupt media, foreigners, bigots, young, old, gay, straight, or any of an endless number of other different demographics. Heck, maybe you're starting to lose sleep over aliens or bigfoot at this point? No matter who you are though, or what ideology you currently subscribe to, odds are you're working longer for less, have less stability in your personal relationships, and increasingly feel like the world is a chaotic, hostile place. Simply put, America isn't working as well as it could be, and so it sort of makes sense that you would want to join a cult (either the Republicans or Democrats) for easy answers.

However, it is actually this two-party system that is the core problem (not aliens). Reforming things to allow more political choice is the most powerful, direct, and fastest solution to all America's ills. And to reiterate, this book is not attempting to take a position on any particular conservative or liberal talking points, but is instead attempting to highlight the basic fallacy in accepting that those should be our only two choices.

Why, for instance, if you believe that abortion is wrong, should you also be required to support unchecked gun ownership with your vote? Or, if you believe in a woman's right to choose abortion, must you necessarily support higher taxes, socialist economics, and gay rights? This book isn't saying which of any of these is "correct", only saying you should be able to make up your own mind on all of them, and vote accordingly. If you honestly think about your preferences, you most likely do not fit into either of the huge red or blue umbrellas that the manipulating two parties at the top want to insist you blindly support. And they don't want you to think about this, because your red versus blue division against your neighbor actually helps keep them both in power.

It is this simplistic, redundant, binary-choice between only Republican or Democrat that has become woefully impotent for dealing with the complexities of our modern world, and is pushing us closer and closer to a systemic crisis we might not recover from. Chris Hedges, a Presbyterian minister, Princeton professor, and Pulitzer Prize-winning foreign correspondent who has firsthand experience seeing countries self-destruct warns in his article "*The Coming Collapse*" that the United States has all the signs of a country falling apart from within.

He wrote, "As a foreign correspondent I covered collapsed societies, including the former Yugoslavia. It is impossible for any doomed population to grasp how fragile the decayed financial, social and political system is on the eve of implosion. All the harbingers of collapse are visible: crumbling infrastructure; chronic underemployment and unemployment; the indiscriminate use of lethal force by police; political paralysis and stagnation; an economy built on the scaffolding of debt; nihilistic mass shootings in schools, universities, workplaces, malls, concert venues and movie theaters; opioid overdoses that kill some 64,000 people a year; an epidemic of suicides; unsustainable military expansion; gambling as a desperate tool of economic development and government revenue; the capture of power by a tiny, corrupt clique; censorship; the physical diminishing of public institutions ranging from schools and libraries to courts and medical facilities; the incessant bombardment by electronic hallucinations to divert us from the depressing sight that has become America and keep us trapped in illusions. We suffer the usual pathologies of impending death. I would be happy to be wrong. But I have seen this before. I know the warning signs. All I can say is get ready."

The first civil war of the 1860s killed over 600,000 Americans, but we need not repeat the horrors of the past, or even create some awful new event. We just need to stop falling for the idea of putting on a red or blue T-shirt that accomplishes nothing except angering your neighbor, while helping a small minority of career politicians and business people get richer.

Instead, let's collectively say no to elephant and donkey group-think alike, and fix our system to operate fairly for everyone with respectful debate, nuanced thinking, and broad participation from all Americans. This book proposes we reform the dysfunctional two-party system currently strangling us into a much more democratic system of multiple viable parties and independent voices.

It is time for a second revolution in America, to prevent things far worse. It will be a peaceful revolution with you as its hero, and the entrenched class of mostly useless, and often corrupt, career-politician Republicans and Democrats as the tyrants who must be overthrown. This is not a revolution to go from capitalist-democracy to socialism, communism, or dictatorship, but a revolution of reform to make America's democracy work for its people like was originally designed. With your help we can renew a functioning government of citizen-politicians like the creators of our country actually envisioned in 1776. And, if you do just as little as sharing the ideas within these pages with people you know, it won't really even be that hard.

Chapter Two

And It Really Is the Two-Party System's Fault
(Or, at least, it wouldn't hurt anything to change it)

But is the current two-party system actually that bad, you might ask? Aren't the two parties passionately opposed to each other, so doesn't one have to be right and the other wrong? And even if our two-party system isn't ideal, having only Republicans and Democrats ever in power is how America is supposed to work, right?

First, no, we're not required by anything to only have Republicans and Democrats to choose from. And second, yes, they both actually suck. It is the two-party system itself—those laws, rules, processes, and disinformation—that the Republicans and Democrats have collectively created over the past few decades, which ensures their own success, while causing most of America's angst and dysfunction. Many people don't realize it, but there is nothing in the Constitution that sanctions or encourages our government always being controlled by only Republican and Democrats. They're both privately run organizations, with no public accountability to any of us, only working to benefit themselves.

Some might immediately argue that your vote is all the accountability the system needs, but in Chapter Four we will explain in detail why this is not actually the case. Far too many Americans have now become utterly complacent in believing the way things are is the only way things can be, and subsequently outsourcing their own thinking to figureheads from these two groups. Even though the term "cult" is used in this book somewhat tongue-in-cheek for the way these groups operate, it's not really that far from the truth. *Psychology Encyclopedia* defines a cult as: "...a structured group, most of whose members demonstrate unquestioned loyalty to a dynamic leader. The cult leader governs most, if not all, aspects of the lives of his or her followers, often insisting that they break all ties with the world outside of the cult."

In fact, three of the United States' founding fathers and first presidents warned of letting our newly formed country fall into a division of just Republicans and Democrats. That's right, only ever having two political parties in control was actually expressly warned against by the exact people who designed how our country was supposed to work.

John Adams (October 2, 1780) stated... "*There is nothing which I dread so much as a division of the republic into two great parties, each arranged under its leader, and concerting measures in opposition to each other. This, in my humble apprehension, is to be dreaded as the greatest political evil...*"

George Washington, our first president, also took time in his final farewell address to warn that political parties "*...are likely in the course of time and things to become potent engines, by which cunning, ambitious, and unprincipled men will be enabled to subvert the power of the people and to usurp for themselves the reins of government...*"

And James Madison, a founding father and president, also presciently warned that breaking the country into two huge political factions would "*divide mankind into rival parties, inflame them with mutual animosity, and render them much more disposed to vex and oppress each other than to cooperate for their common good.*"

Sound familiar? Simply put, our democracy was never designed to work with only two parties and its tearing the country apart.

But, even if you think that is just the opinion of some old, dead, white guys that no longer matter, consider what one of the most prestigious universities in the modern world, Harvard, found. In their extensive 2017 political study, *Why Competition in the Politics Industry is Failing America*, Harvard University determined that most of our current issues really are from having only these two political options. The authors of the 2017 political study (Gehl and Porter) explain, "It's important to recognize that much of what constitutes today's political system has no basis in the Constitution. As our system evolved, the parties—and a larger political industrial complex that surrounds them—established and optimized a set of rules and practices that enhanced their power and diminished our democracy." We strongly recommend you read the full Harvard study for free online or listen to a great, hour-long interview with the authors on Freakonomics Radio episode 356 as they summarize it.

The core of their findings is that lack of real competition is the main issue within our current two-party system of governance. They continue, "Rivalry in a duopoly is almost always constrained, because the two rivals recognize that head-to-head competition is mutually destructive... They will both benefit from an 'attractive' industry (as defined from their perspective)—one that strengthens and reinforces their way of competing, limits the power of other actors, and increases barriers to entry. In a duopoly, rivals will also cooperate (or collude) to enhance the industry in their favor and avoid undermining it."

They go on to explain, "Competing on division reinforces the parties' artificial divisions, and the parties seek to reinforce these divisions through confusion and by misleading voters on the facts about what they should actually want... The duopoly avoids compromise. Party rhetoric divides voters based on hostility toward the other side. Rather than working to bring citizens together to further the public interest, each party demonizes the other party's supporters and their views. The duopoly incites citizens to vote based on anger and fear...The real problem is that our political system is no longer designed to serve the public interest, but them and their industry allies."

Those. Bastards. So, instead of real competition, Republicans and Democrats have created a kabuki theater-like rivalry that does nothing to solve America's problems but only ensures their own power. That last political fight you got in with your uncle at Thanksgiving, the one that made your date "see you differently," was actually an orchestrated tool to facilitate some rich Washington politico's summer home purchase.

But, okay, you might now say, even if having just two political parties isn't ideal, we've still got the greatest democracy on earth, right, so if it ain't broke, why fix it? Well... because it is broke (did you not read Chapter One?). To get a grasp of the actual damage our two-party system is doing to us, let's look at the independent conclusions of another political study from Princeton University. Princeton's own 2014 political study concluded that the US is actually no longer even a functioning democracy. Looking at regular voters' actual impact on policy, the Princeton study frighteningly concluded the US has already crept into the classification of being an oligarchy. They found the will of America's voters has been almost completely superseded by a small group of wealthy business moguls entrenched with politicians.

The Princeton authors (Gilens and Page) declare, "The central point that emerges from our research is that economic elites and organized groups representing business interests have substantial independent impacts on U.S. government policy, while mass-based interest groups and average citizens have little or no independent influence." Let that sink in. America is no longer a functioning democracy, but an oligarchy. Like Russia, or arguably China or North Korea. Yikes, that ain't good, dawg.

If you'd like a great explanation of how little your opinion actually matters to the passing of public policy in modern America, take ten minutes to watch Represent.Us' "Unbreaking America," starring Jennifer Lawrence, for free on their website. This utter breakdown in our democracy would have been far less likely to have happened, if decades ago we had stopped allowing just two private groups to have all the power without any real competition. However, we can wake up and make it better now.

The whole point of America's democracy is that you, the citizen, are to dictate its function. In fact, according to the Constitution, the government only gets its limited powers by being loaned from you over a temporary period of time. You are the true first owner of political power in America, not royalty, the rich, or certain individuals who weasel their way into political careers (both those elected and lobbyists). This idea of your inherent "popular sovereignty" was exactly what our founding fathers risked their lives to achieve, and then warned against us ever losing with a lazy slide into a dysfunctional system of two not-so-different parties always sharing control. Although it's a slightly more complicated idea to grasp, today's enemy is not the next standard-bearer the Republicans and Democrats each prop up on election time for you to hate (buying into that actually helps them), but it is our two-party system itself.

As political activist and professor Lawrence Lessig deftly emphasizes in his book *Republic, Lost*, "there is probably no one single evil character or person we can all rally behind as the villain in our modern dilemma (as easy as that would be), but the problem is that the faulty, corrupted structure has now become entrenched and self-fulfilling. We aren't living in a dangerous tyranny we have seen before, but in a new dark time where the rational conclusion of morally absent capitalist democracy is systemically nearing the point where John Adams cautioned, 'all democracies eventually commit suicide.'"

Like a cancer eating its host, the problems of the two-party system we now lazily accept as a "given" have become too systemic for any elected good people within either existing political party to make a positive dent. Is there one really evil, old rich guy in a gold-platted tower cackling maniacally as he pulls the strings over all this dysfunction and corruption? Maybe, but probably not. Unfortunately when a system morphs into one of near monopolistic control, you don't need a single super villain, it is self-perpetuating. So, the first step in changing the two-party system is for us to become aware of it, and stop buying into it. It's time to stop yelling over red and blue, and deal with that incredibly dysfunctional elephant (and its donkey friend) in the room. Our modern American political system has essentially morphed into a corrupted and ineffectual oligarchy that can provide no leadership, nor achieve anything, except making the most corrupt individuals richer. And if the two-party system is the disease rotting us from within, then the best democratic-based cure is obvious.

Competition.

Just like in business, real competition to the Republicans and Democrats through independent voices and political groups, is the answer. And this competition will naturally occur, once we simply undo the steps the two parties have collectively taken to insulate themselves from it.

Chapter Three

But We Can Fix It
(Or, at least, make it a lot better)

So, the answer to America's core problem is more political competition. The two-party system needs competition to keep them honest and functioning, and we need competition amongst political ideas to calm the growing division between ourselves and our neighbors. In short, we all need to help there be more options than just red versus blue. A system of more open political thought, maybe even a working multiparty system, to provide alternate political parties and independent candidates without Republican or Democratic ties an actual chance to win and govern, is the best way to save you, me, and all of America.

But maybe your all-American, gun-toting, transgender hairdresser Burt insists it could never work in America. Well, it could be he's exactly the sort of myopic, lazy thinker that keeps us perpetually stuck each election. Creating a multiparty system in the US, or at least increasing the odds of independent politicians getting elected, is not impossible, it's actually more natural than restricting everything to only two groups. And, correcting our system would be as simple as making yourself and your friends aware of those very laws, rules, and protocols —explained throughout the rest of this book—that the Republicans and Democrats have purposely set up trying to insulate themselves. A recent Pew Research Center study even indicated Americans are already primed to support eight political parties, we just haven't collectively known how to get there yet. This book hopefully starts the roadmap.

The thought of having a multiparty system may seem overwhelming to some Americans, but that's probably just because they don't really know what it would entail. At its core it would just mean improving our system to allow more people a fair chance of winning office without having to be pre-approved by the current Republican and Democratic gate-keepers. We wouldn't be forcing political involvement from people who aren't actually winning elections, but simply removing the artificial barriers that currently don't allow them to. The eventual natural result would be more parties to choose from, and more independent-thinking politicians winning elections.

Multiparty systems are being used successfully in many modern industrialized democracies around the world. Certainly, some—Germany, Canada, the UK, and Israel—work better than others—such as Italy—but as Mark Schmitt confirms in his 2016 Vox article, almost any additional truly viable US parties, "...would not only give citizens a chance to express their views in the voting booth but would also open up the system and create new alliances and bargains, breaking down the sense of two well-fortified, unmoving camps."

And before your hairdresser Burt grumbles something else about, "But we're 'Muricans, we don't want to be like them," keep in mind there are no set rules on how a political system has to work. We can make a multiparty system however we want, the initial step is simply to remove the purposefully-created barriers that help Republicans and Democrats avoid competition, then more independents and third-party candidates will quickly start to show up. We can debate and fine tune how a new multiparty American system can best function as we move forward with it.

Realistically, we should still only expect to have two or three core parties winning the greatest portion of government control at any time for the immediate future, but even that's okay. Just having the viable addition of independent party ideals being debated on a national scale forces the larger ones to listen and negotiate to form more moderate coalitions capable of governing. It would move everything from the extremes toward a moderate center. Even just ten percent of our future Congress being consistently non-Republican and

Democrat would deal a serious blow to vitriolic, binary thinking of red versus blue in politicians and ourselves. If, like in Israel, there are up to a dozen competitive parties in each election with nuanced views on every issue from abortion to terrorism to taxation, it would be much harder to convince the public to angrily side with either just the right or the left. And, once the two-party entrenchment is weakened, the corrupt oligarchic system of money buying favorable legislation will lose some of its grip as well.

With fresh and diverse paths to power, and new political parties suddenly resonating with their particular ideals, more citizens will become engaged in political decision-making than ever before. Political anger and polarization will begin naturally reducing. That's the way competition works in business, and it can work in the business of politics too. If the Republicans and Democrats really have the best ideas, they should be able to handle the heat of real competition.

To create this lasting change to the system and bring real multiparty competition to the Republicans and Democrats, we must do two things. First, we must change the way our political leaders are elected (election reform) at the federal, state, and local levels, into a more fair, honest, and inclusive process for voices not affiliated with the Republicans or Democrats. Second, we must alter the current system of governance (governing reform) to lessen the two-party's corrupt control over whoever gets elected. Luckily, these are both remarkably achievable.

The next section of the book, "The Solutions," spells out in detail what YOUR specific actions can be to create lasting change. Each section covers a separate, but important issue it would help to correct, and the specific things you might do to help. There are also additional, more general, actions suggested at the end of each chapter. Keep in mind, if you've got the print copy of this book, you might have to do a little more work actually googling the websites or information mentioned, but if you have the ebook, direct links to resources are provided whenever possible. This book in no way claims to be the originator of most of these ideas, but simply stands on the shoulders of countless political thinkers, reformers, and activists before it. This book only aspires to be a functional tool which compiles the best of these ideas to facilitate discussion and action.

You should also be aware there are intelligent differences of opinions on what the most urgent aspects of political reform are, even between those who are already convinced change is necessary. For instance, the terrific group FairVote.org sees bringing structural changes for better competition to congressional races as the most important first step, while the author Lawrence Lessig cites money's influence in our national politics as the root cause of all our dysfunction. Whether you see election laws, lobbying, gerrymandering, the electoral college, morality, or even the Republicans or Democrats (one side, but not the other) being the primary culprit for our anemic government, our goal shouldn't be to waste time arguing an airtight case for which is the worst. We should instead be helping facilitate and encourage ALL the positive changes possible right now, without letting hypothetical perfection stop us from implementing any improvements today.

The two-party system is a multi-headed hydra stretching its tentacles throughout local, state, and federal governments, with Republican and Democratic corruption and dysfunction slithering from the Supreme Court to Congress to the White House and even into our own minds. It is urgent we stop its growth with multiple points of attack. It is time to not only move on from the function of two-party rule but grow into new ideologies and practices. The important thing is for you to do something now. Just jump into whatever chapter seems most interesting or important to you, and find something you can do. Heck, even just reading this much and being able to talk to someone about it, or pass this book on, will help spread the knowledge. You can also sign up at Independ.Me and subscribe to the "Independ Me" youtube channel.

Imagine, fellow American, in the very near future you are able to vote for a political leader who represents all your ideals and is someone you can trust. Fundamental and systemic change to our political system is the way forward, not just once again hoping that voting between the "lesser of two evils" will miraculously improve things, even though it never has before. Great things can happen, if you just do your part to start this second American revolution.

Let's begin...

Part Two

The Solutions

"I hold it that a little rebellion now and then is a good thing, and as necessary in the political world as storms in the physical."

—Thomas Jefferson

Chapter Four

Freeing Our Congress from Polarization and Corruption

While creating the House of Representatives, John Adams said it was to be "*an exact portrait of the people at large.*" It's a shame that's not the way it works. In recent decades both houses of Congress have degenerated into partisan, corrupt, unrepresentative, and dysfunctional wastes of citizen time and money. In their current form, they have actually become a major hindrance to our functioning democracy.

Our Constitution lays out far more governing power to the Congress than the president. Congress was given the power to create all laws, control the federal budget, declare war, and make peace through those people that we, the American citizens, collectively choose to represent us. Congress is therefore supposed to be the heart of our democracy, not the president or the courts, so it is imperative that we fix it to function the way it was designed.

Problems with our Congress are primarily twofold. First, congressional elections have become dramatically undemocratic, arguably even rigged, by the main two parties to create a government that is absolutely no longer representative of the entirety of America's citizens. Second, once those less than ideal, non-representative people get elected to Congress, they inevitably govern poorly, by consistently putting loyalty to their political party—and in turn lobbyist money—over the country's needs.

In regards to the first issue of rigged elections, how scary would it be if the House of Representative elections were so orchestrated by the controlling two parties that upwards of 80 percent of their outcomes could be predicted over a year in advance, regardless of knowing your vote, or even who the actual candidates were yet? Well, FairVote.org was able to do precisely this in 2016, because most of the time your vote doesn't actually matter that much in our currently biased system. In its fascinating study, *Monopoly Politics*, FairVote.org explains, "The outcome of more than 80 percent of U.S. House races can be predicted with near certainty years ahead of the election. In 2012 and 2014 House elections, our model made "high-confidence" projections in 701 contests (80.5 percent of all races), and was correct in all but one. Two days after the 2014 elections we issued our high-confidence projections for 2016 in five of six races with 100 percent accuracy."

Wow. Just... wow. This means that even if you wanted to elect someone into Congress who wasn't going to blindly support either the Republican or Democratic party like a goose-stepping zombie, your vote couldn't even do it these days. Each individual election has already been predestined through closed primaries, gerrymandering (the two parties redrawing congressional districts to make as many uncompetitive as possible), and the corrupt single-winner congressional election system the Republicans and Democrats have colluded on making law across the country. And then once elected, those mostly party-picked sycophants do a repugnant job of executing their actual responsibilities to you and the country.

Consider, new members of Congress are required to put their hands over their hearts and take the following oath for our country's well-being: "*I do solemnly swear that I will support and defend the Constitution of the United States against all enemies, foreign and domestic; that I will bear true faith and allegiance to the same; that I take this obligation freely, without any mental reservation or purpose of evasion; and that I will well and faithfully discharge the duties of the office on which I am about to enter: So help me God.*"

Unfortunately, a rare minority of them take that oath seriously, if you look objectively at their actions. The Constitution is largely concerned with protecting your rights and the separation of powers in government, but as former

Congressman Mikey Edwards, cofounder of the terrific reform organization *No Labels* and author of *The Parties Versus the People*, writes, "they begin dividing into rival camps on the very day they are sworn into office." The fact is, the vast majority of modern Congressmen and women immediately begin disregarding their above oath to the Constitution, and their fiduciary responsibility to you who voted for them, in near-treasonous fashion as soon as their hand drops in favor of their party. "In the House of Representatives, the division into warring camps begins the very first hour of a member's service," Congressman Edwards explains.

Even if an occasional independent-thinking person slips into the system the two controlling political parties, and their closely entwined lobbyists, still won't allow them to buck their corrupt and dysfunctional party standards. David Davenport's Dec 13, 2017 *Forbes* article explains how congressional party-line voting has soared in the last forty years from about 60 percent in the 1970s to a consistent 90 percent now. This brainwashed party conformity is systemic within a governmental body which was once considered the most deliberative in the world, the shining light of democracy on earth. Clearly it now has no "deliberation" whatsoever, as every member has already put on their red or blue T-shirt immediately after lying their way through their oath. They aren't YOUR representative; they are automatons of the two parties, exactly like the founding fathers warned against so long ago. The enemy has become the collective two-party entrenchment and those people they get elected.

Mr. Edwards goes on to write, "Too often our elected leaders seem to think of themselves not as trustees of America's future, but as members of a political club... Meanwhile our bridges grow old and collapse, our banks and investment houses pursue policies that cripple our economy, and we become ever more dependent on Chinese money and middle east oil."

So ask yourself, in a system where your vote for who is

elected doesn't matter, then those "elected" don't take their responsibilities to the Constitution or you seriously, but instead vote with their lobbyist-dictated party 90 percent of the time, where is the democracy? Nonexistent, that's where.

Luckily, the solution to removing the polarization and corruption from this branch of our government is fairly straightforward, coming largely in two parts. First, *Section A* of this chapter on election reform will show four things you can do to correct the skewed and corrupted makeup of Congress to assure better, more representative, and independent-thinking people are elected who are not already indoctrinated to only Republican or Democratic loyalty. Second, *Section B* on governing reform, shows four steps that can be taken to help Congress govern in a nonpartisan way outside of two-party pressure, once new independent-thinking, representative individuals are elected.

Both of these concerns are important to permanently solve our modern issues, but as is stated repeatedly in this book you shouldn't feel overwhelmed in doing everything. Any of these actions are better than nothing, and other tactics for addressing lobbying corruption, the presidential election, and polarization of the courts will be handled in subsequent chapters. Enhancing Congress' ability to function the way it was originally designed is possibly the most direct route to restoring American democracy, however, and therefore should be on the top of any list of reforms.

Section A) How to Make Congressional Elections More Fair

Congress A1: *Change Congressional Elections to Multi-Winner-Districts with Ranked Choice Voting (called Fair Representation)*

This may sound like a lot and/or confusing at first glance, but it is really not. And this solution is listed first as it is probably the single-most impactful for the entire United States. If you read or do nothing else, please try to grasp this issue and fight for its implementation, even if it's just by mentioning it to other people. The biggest hurdle is in simply helping people to understand the difference between how our current system works and how it would be much improved—more democratic and less corrupt—by implementing Fairvote.org's Fair Representation plan.

The dysfunctional system we have now, which was largely jointly entrenched by the Republicans and Democrats in their 1967 law, *The Uniform Congressional District Act*, is a single-winner-district, winner-take-all format. This single-winner-district format with winner-take-all vote tallying is the core reason our Congress does not accurately represent America's population as it was designed to. The current system is only ideal for supporting the corrupted two parties, not actual democracy.

As FairVote.org explains, "most elections in the United States are winner-take-all: instead of reflecting all voters, our legislators reflect only the biggest or strongest group of voters that elected them, leaving all others unrepresented. The use of winner-take-all voting methods in our elections for state legislatures and Congress is a central reason for major problems with our politics: gerrymandering, partisan gridlock, no-choice elections and distortions in fair representation all have roots in the inherent problems of winner-take-all methods." Alternatively, Fair Representation is essentially FairVote's brilliantly Americanized proportional representation system, combined with ranked-choice-voting, and it would correct these issues. If you'd like an excellent, easy-to-understand explanation on how multi-winner districts with ranked-choice voting would be an improvement to our current system without having to read, just spend a few minutes on FairVote.org/videos page or search for "Fairvote's Fair Representation" on Youtube or Google. We'll go ahead and summarize the basics right here as well though.

In our currently failing, single-winner-districts, each voter only votes for one potential representative, almost always a choice between only the party-chosen Republican and Democratic candidates. The winner of any congressional district is chosen by getting the most—a plurality—of the vote in that district, while the loser gets nothing. This current system of voting between only two candidates for a single seat to represent you gives 51 percent of the voters 100 percent of the power, and 49 percent of the voters 0 percent of the power. Certainly, the winners of elections should be occupying congressional seats, and any party with a majority of representatives should win majority control of the House or Senate as makes sense in a democracy, however, the rest of America should ideally still be represented proportionately, not completely shut out. Even if everyone in a given congressional district was happily split into either Republican or Democratic camps—which they absolutely are not—it is still inherently unrepresentative of a huge portion of the population (the half that loses). Not only is this corrupt system less than ideally democratic as the Constitution dictates Congress to function, but it also creates the awful argument of a third-party vote being "wasted." The ability to overthrow the chosen two-party winner is a mathematical improbability in our current single-winner system, thereby strengthening the red and blue propaganda-supported idea of "strategic voting" (wasting your vote on the "lesser of two evils") than voting for someone you actually respect and ideologically agree with. Over time, this system necessarily ends up gravitating toward only ever producing two viable alternatives within a voting block, continually reinforcing the political landscape being split into two large, dysfunctional, and happily corrupt parties, rather than giving a free and open arena of many distinct political voices and ideologies focused on solving all of Americas' problems.

In most multiparty systems within Europe, proportional representation is achieved through voters having to cast their ballots for a party rather than an individual. However, this goes against the superior American ideal of voters being able to choose a particular individual to represent them in government. FairVote.org has ingeniously devised a way to get multi-winner districts in the US, through achieving the same benefits while keeping direct representation.

Their Fair Representation system will work by: 1) having each voting district elect multiple representatives rather than just one, and 2) implementing ranked-choice-voting ballots to essentially remove the ability for any third-party vote to be "wasted." All states could easily do this, without increasing the number of representatives in Congress, by combining their smaller districts into larger ones (and do away with the problem of gerrymandering in the process), thereby keeping the total number of representatives in Congress the same. Multi-winner districts immediately create a scenario where third-party and independent candidates have a much greater mathematical chance of winning. And again, if you want a quick and easy way to understand the Fair Representation concept with visuals just go to fairvote.org's website and watch their video.

As Paul David Miller writes in his June 1, 2016 *Federalist* article, "Switching to proportional representation at the state and national level would be the most significant change to our system of government since the Civil War, if not the Constitutional Convention. Such a change would fundamentally alter American politics, catalyzing the most sweeping and fundamental realignment in American history." He goes on to state that the change would necessarily lead to more parties, more democracy, and more honesty in government.

The second part of Fair Representation, ranked-choice-voting, only means that instead of being forced to vote for only one candidate, voters would rank preferences of potential candidates from first to last. For example, if a newly combined multi-winner district in a state had four candidates, your ballot would allow you to rank each candidate from one through four in your preference order for who wins. A computerized system would compile all ballots through instant runoffs on election day, whereby if your first choice is mathematically eliminated your vote is automatically applied to your next choice until a winner is found. You can check out a more thorough breakdown of how it works at ballotpedia.org/ranked-choice-voting_(RCV). Although this may seem complex at first glance, it is used extensively around the world for many contests, including the Oscars in the United States. It would allow everyone to vote for other parties and individuals rather than only the Republican and Democratic chosen candidates without fear of wasting their vote, and it ensures the greatest number of Americans being happy with the use of their vote.

As Howard Dean stated in his October 7, 2016 New York Times op-ed regarding RCV, "Voters can support their favorites while still voting effectively against their least favorite. Having more competition encourages better dialogue on issues. Civility is substantially improved. Needing to reach out to more voters leads candidates to reduce personal attacks and govern more inclusively."

With this singular change to Fair Representation elections for Congress (simultaneously implementing multi-winner districts and ranked-choice-voting), we could take a massive leap toward making sure government is more representative of actual Americans as the Constitution dictates. It will also ensure voters have more ability to choose a winner that matches their ideals. This change would immediately begin populating Congress with people who are not already predetermined to participate in polarizing vitriol for the Republicans' and Democrats' sake. It is the most ideal way to foster a system where multiple parties have a chance to take hold, yet we can protect and even enhance the American ideal of directly electing your chosen representative.

Luckily, after much research and organization, FairVote.org has got a bill called the *Fair Representation Act (HR 4000)* introduced to the 116th Congress by Representative Donald Beyer. FairVote.org explains in their report *Monopoly Politics*, "The Fair Representation Act would require Representatives to be elected by ranked choice voting. It would require that every state with more than one seat elect its Representatives in multi-winner elections; states with five or fewer seats would elect all statewide while those with more would draw multi-winner districts, each electing between three and five winners. Finally, it would require that the larger states that use districts adopt an independent redistricting commission to create the district map."

FairVote goes on to predict the multi-winner ranked-choice voting changes made with the *Fair Representation Act* would singlehandedly "triple the number of Americans able to participate in House elections that are competitive between the two major parties." And, "the use of ranked choice voting and the lower thresholds for election make it possible for candidates outside the two major parties to compete on a level playing field and hold the major parties accountable."

The bill represents the most straightforward and powerful way for the positive changes becoming mandatory for House of Representative elections. Tips for how you can immediately begin supporting it are listed below.

So, what you should do? Any or all of the following...

1) Support passing the Fair Representation Act into law. Watch a quick video explaining the Fair Representation Act on FairVote.org and sign an online petition supporting it.

2) Directly email or call all your representatives. Believe it or not, you putting pressure on your current representatives does have an impact, even if you are just one voice. And thanks to Azavea's technology (located at https://live.cicerodata.com), you can literally find the phone numbers and emails of everyone who represents you in all forms of government for free within about five seconds. Contact your representatives and tell them you want them to support the *Fair Representation Act H.R. 4000* of the 116th Congress becoming law.

Key Section Takeaways

Fair Representation (or something like it) would stop Republicans and Democrats from being the only ones who can get elected to Congress.

It would allow ALL Americans proportional representation in Congress through a combination of multi-winner districts and ranked choice voting

Congress A2: *Change All Closed Primaries to Open (Top Two) Nonpartisan Primaries*

This is arguably the second most important action for breaking the two-party system and allowing independents to truly compete. Whether for congressional seats, governorships, local offices or president, closed primaries are a horrible thing for the citizenry of America and our democracy. They only serve to reinforce the corrupt system of Republican and Democratic rule. In some cases, they literally allow the most extremely polarized 5 percent of our population to pick the only candidates in consideration for the more moderate 95 percent of America on election day. Sadly, our system has developed whereby primaries are now arguably the only elections that actually "matter," yet in the vast majority of cases only party loyalists are allowed to vote in them. Closed primaries solely controlled by private institutions known as the Republicans and Democrats were not even imagined as enough of a real possibility by the founding fathers to warn against, but now epitomize their greatest fears. They simply shouldn't exist.

The powerful 2017 Harvard political report, *Why Competition in the Politics Industry is Failing America*, even stated, "the current partisan primary system is perhaps the single most powerful obstacle to achieving outcomes for the common good. Instead, states should move to a single primary ballot for all candidates no matter what their affiliation, and open up primaries to all voters, not just registered party voters."

Ironically, closed primaries came into existence in the early twentieth century as a way to lessen back room party deals crowning candidates and to instead allow more direct voting influence by concerned citizens. Now though, those decent original intentions have morphed into a system where only the most extreme and partisan Republicans and

Democrats (the ones who typically vote in closed primaries) are the sole gatekeepers deciding which few candidates are ever even in consideration for election by the general public. They completely exclude independents (over one-third of the US population) from the earliest, and arguably most important, part of the election process. Whenever a moderate or independent thinker even attempts to run for office, it is highly unlikely he or she will make it through the currently biased primary process to ever possibly get elected by the moderate majority who would have most likely supported them. And, it is important to reiterate that the Republican and Democratic parties controlling these primaries are both private institutions, not at all sanctioned by the Constitution or any true oversight. They are unsurprisingly working toward their own benefit.

As Brian Dickerson explains for *The Detroit Free Press*, the closed primary system is rigged against the middle: "We like to believe that partisan primaries are the political equivalent of the playoffs that take place each fall in Major League Baseball's National and American leagues, yielding each league's strongest contender for the World Series. But that's not how the partisan primary system works. Not surprisingly, the relative handful of voters who turn out for the partisan primaries in which both major parties choose their nominees for gubernatorial and congressional races is much smaller, and much more partisan, than the larger electorate that participates in the November general election. ...A fiscally conservative Democratic candidate or a pro-choice Republican might appeal to the large and diverse November electorate. But neither has much chance of surviving the partisan vetting process that would earn them a place on the November ballot. It's as if the strongest team in the National League were disqualified from participating in the World Series because it had too many fans in American League cities."

And as Mikey Edwards in *The Parties Versus the People* writes, "We Americans believe in choice. In almost every facet of our lives from soups to soaps to stereos, we expect, and demand, multiple options. How strange it is that in the area that counts far more than any of these, and that determines how much we will pay in taxes, what government services we will receive, and even whether our sons or daughters or husbands or wives will be sent off to fight and possibly die on a foreign battlefield, we allow two private organizations whose primary goal is the gaining and keeping of power to tell us on election day that we are allowed to choose only between the two people they have told us we must choose between."

Should we really continue to allow two private, extremist, corrupt institutions to pick the only two people you are allowed to vote for? Luckily, the solution is fairly straightforward. As openprimaries.org shows in their terrific two-minute video, the answer is to simply do away with party-controlled closed primaries, in all states, for open primaries. An open primary in any given state would allow all candidates meeting a basic threshold of support—petition signatures to keep out the least viable individuals—to run regardless of party affiliation. Additionally, everyone in the given state would be allowed to participate in voting without having to be a member of a party. The top two strongest candidates would then move on to the general election for that state, regardless of whether or not they were Republicans, Democrats, a third party, or completely unaffiliated. This solution is straightforward, entirely more representative and democratic than our current system, and full of common sense. And once again, a bill has already been structured and sponsored, all you need to do it is support it becoming a law.

Congressman John Delaney sponsored the *Open Our Democracy Act (H.R. 2981)* in the 115th Congress in 2017. If it had been passed into law, it would have instituted an open primary for federal races, created independent redistricting commissions in each state, and made Election Day a federal holiday. This act becoming law would represent a straightforward federal change that some states like (2010) California and (2004) Washington have already begun to implement. Although there are some other bills proposed in the 116th Congress that contains parts of the Open Our Democracy Act goals, it would be helpful to bring this proposed legislation back for consideration in this, and any future Congress, until it becomes law. At the time of this book's publication, Representative Fitzpatrick's HR 163 CLEAN Elections Act seems like the closest, both requiring open primaries and dealing with issues of gerrymandering. Additionally, this is an issue that can be addressed very effectively on the state level as well, by putting pressure on your state legislature to do away with closed primaries, if your state still has them. It's time to end closed primaries on both the federal and state levels and take a huge chunk of power back from the red and blue shirt wearers.

So, what you should do? Any or all of the following...

1) Sign up at openprimaries.org and give your support to a new version of the Open Our Democracy Act, geared toward bringing open primaries to every state in the country. You can also check out their helpful map to see the current status of primaries in your state, and movements to help rectify the situation. Through their website you can even contact your representatives and local movements.

2) Go to Change.org to start a petition (or a citizen's initiative if your state allows) for doing away with closed primaries. Each state has its own rules and processes for starting a citizen's initiative (See Chap 9, Sec 8), but regardless, if there is not already an active movement in your area you can get the ball rolling by easily starting a petition at change.org. Get momentum by sending it out over social media for support prior to delivering it to your chosen governmental recipients.

3) Contact your Congressional representatives (https://live.cicerodata.com) to tell them to support the *CLEAN Elections Act (HR 163)* in the 116th Congress.

Key Section Takeaways

Closed primaries are bad, benefiting only the most extreme Republicans and Democrats

Open primaries anywhere will help lessen polarization, and increase the odds of moderates and independents getting elected

Congress A3: *Eliminate Unjust "Sore Loser" Laws, and the 1967 Uniform Congressional District Act*

There are essentially two laws, one federal and the other prevalent in many states under different names, that hinder the ability of third parties and independents getting elected across the country. The federal law is the 1967 *Uniform Congressional District Act*, and the other is a version of the "sore loser" law that's been adopted by forty states.

The 1967 *Uniform Congressional District Act* outlawed any congressional district from being multi-winner. It universally forced all districts across the country to be single-winner, winner-take-all in a fashion that drastically benefits only Republicans and Democrats staying in power. It effectively squashes any efforts for states to use any form of the more democratic models mentioned above (section A1). If the *Fair Representation Act* is voted into law, it will successfully make the *Uniform Congressional District Act* moot. However, separate repeal pressure of the law would still be immensely helpful in allowing states to pursue their own efforts of creating a fairer electoral system. Ever since the 1967 law was passed by Congress, third parties have experienced a drastic reduction in their ability to provide true competition to Republicans and Democrats.

As Michael Colbenz writes about elections prior to 1967 in *The Hill*, "Was there something different then that allowed these third parties to exist? Yes, multi-seat Congressional Districts. A multi-seat district could have two or more elected representatives. This system allowed a candidate to be elected with as little as 10 percent of the vote. This allowed candidates from minor parties to win office, which allowed these parties to gain political traction and eventually participate in a meaningful way on the national stage. Our current single seat districts, with 'winner-take-all' elections, favors parties that can assemble coalitions of over fifty percent of the voters. This favors the two major parties... Congress eliminated multi-seat districts in 1967 with the passage of the *Uniform Congressional Districts Act*. It is time to repeal this law. It is time to give the American people a meaningful choice in politics."

Any federal law can be removed by simply getting over 50 percent of the members of Congress to vote for it to be repealed. By everyone putting pressure on their individual representatives in the House and Senate we could force them to repeal his two-party-loving law, and finally open up the chances of multiple parties once again mattering in the United States, whether or not more comprehensive Fair Representation legislation is ever passed. This can be achieved by all of us sending emails, texts and phone messages to our congressmen demanding they do it, or by the more formal process of a citizen's initiative (Chap 9, Sec 8).

Additionally, many "sore-loser laws" in states work hand in hand with closed primaries and gerrymandering to eliminate true competition for the corrupted two parties. Over forty states in the US have "sore-loser" laws in place that basically forbid any candidate from running as a third-party or independent once they have failed to win either a Republican or Democratic primary. This sets a horrible conundrum for any independent-thinking candidate. He or she must essentially try to win either a Republican or Democratic closed primary to run in the general election for a reasonable chance of winning. However, if they do not win that primary, they are then banned from legally still running as an independent. In every sense of the concept this is undemocratic, and only serves to benefit the two corrupt parties always in power, the very ones who have created these laws across the country.

As Michael Kang from Emory University states, "Party polarization occurs because the party voters with more extreme ideological preferences control their party primaries and elect more extreme candidates as the major party nominees. Party voters screen out more moderate candidates, who have no recourse under sore loser laws other than to become more ideologically extreme in pursuit of primary success. In the absence of a sore loser law, however, party dissenters can threaten a sore loser run that should worry the party's nominees about splitting the base during the general election. As a result, a repeal of sore loser laws should encourage party leaders and party nominees to reach effective compromises with important dissenting elements within the party to stave off these threats. If they do not, then moderate candidates who cannot survive the primary are free to challenge the major party nominees from the political center in the general election."

Even without primaries or gerrymandering eliminated, repealing sore-loser laws in as many states as possible will absolutely lead to more moderates, independents, and third-party candidates getting elected. It would even force Republicans and Democrats to consider catering to a broader audience than the most extreme ideologues within their groups. Beating the corrupt two-party system requires a multi-pronged approach to be successful, and we should fight both of these biased laws that serve to protect the two entrenched parties at the same time as any other steps.

So what you should do? Any or all of the following...

1) In addition to supporting the *Fair Representation Act* mentioned in Section A1, you can also start your own petition to get the *Uniform Congressional District Act* repealed. Go to Change.org to start a petition (or a citizen's initiative if your state allows) for doing away with closed primaries. A citizen's initiative (Chap 9, Sec 8) is a petition that formally forces a legislative body to convene and vote on an issue. The free online generator at change.org will not only allow you to easily draft a petition, but also get momentum by sending it out over social media prior to delivering it to your chosen governmental recipients. This can be a powerful tool in addressing the repeal of whatever specific sore loser laws may exist in your own state.

2) Email or call your state representatives, and tell them you want any "sore loser" laws in your state repealed. Use the free technology located at https://live.cicerodata.com to immediately find them. As this is primarily state-based legislature, contacting your state representatives to tell them you are concerned about this issue will be the most impactful. You can even use all or part of the email template located in Appendix 1 to send to them.

3) Consider joining SAM. SAM in a new independent political group that has, amongst many other great goals to end two-party corruption and dysfunction, a strategy for repealing sore loser laws around the country. Go to joinsam.org to check them out.

Key Section Takeaways

The federal Uniform Congressional Districts Act ensures ongoing two party control and needs to be repealed

Your individual state probably has a "sore loser" law making it harder for independents to get elected. It also needs to be repealed

Congress A4: *Eliminate Gerrymandering*

"Gerrymandering" is a pretty fucking weird word, and it often scares people off from understanding how stopping the practice would be a huge help in breaking the corrupted two party system's control of our government. If you want a detailed, yet straightforward, explanation of gerrymandering we'd suggest you start with Christopher Ingraham's helpful *Washington Post* article from March 1, 2015. The basics are that gerrymandering is the term for when Republicans or Democrats in power redraw congressional district lines (redistricting) with bias to help facilitate winning future races, regardless of how those changes affect the concept of Congress fairly representing all Americans.

Depending on who you listen to, Republicans or Democrats are accused of doing it more. The truth is that they both absolutely do it as much as they can, whenever they are in a position of power to do it. Redistricting itself is a necessary process that a democracy must do every so often to attempt to make representation as ideal as possible, but the "gerrymandering" version of it is when it's done with biased intent to keep those with power in power. In the process, it once again violates that core principle John Adams mentioned earlier of Congress being intended as an "*exact representation of the people*." Sometimes the Republicans get a slight advantage from gerrymandering, sometimes the Democrats, but the absolute perpetual losers are any moderates, independents, or third-party candidates, as well as Americans on the whole, since Congress inevitably doesn't accurately represent us.

The main thing to know about gerrymandering is that it sucks, corrupts the necessary process of appropriate redistricting, and it needs to stop. It is largely agreed that the best way to prevent this corruption is by completely taking redistricting power out of the hands of the politicians benefiting from it and giving it to an independent system. Policymap.com has a great summary of a couple of the most promising solutions in their 2017 "Solutions to Gerrymandering" article, as well as there being myriad federal and state bills proposed to supposedly fix it. Some of these proposed laws are better than others. With many, unfortunately, just superficially shifting the power of redistricting to people who are still loyal to the Republicans and Democrats. So, it's important to learn the specifics of any bill or candidate proposing a solution before supporting it.

Laws on how, and by whom, congressional district maps get drawn are typically done on a state-by-state basis, meaning there are a lot of ways gerrymandering is enabled around the country. This also means state action is a particularly effective way to enact change on this issue. A terrific resource to get up to speed on these issues and potential solutions is the Brennan Center for Justice (brennancenter.org), where you can find up to date information for most gerrymandering court cases and developments, as well as an amazing interactive map that shows you what federal and state legislation you can support based on where you live. Once you look at the sheer number of proposed legislative solutions in states and a national basis (22 national proposals in the 116th Congress alone so far), you will start to see the complexity of which solutions to support.

That said, you might want to contacting your federal representatives to tell them to support Rep Brian Fitzpatrick's *HR 163 CLEAN Elections Act*. It appears to be a straightforward bill proposed in the 116th Congress to require states to both turn over redistricting to independent commissions, as well as have open primaries. You can also check out Represent.Us' efforts to get their *American Anti-Corruption Act* (you can find out more about this Act and movement in Chapter Four's money section as well as the Cool Ideas in Chapter Nine) through local and state means, which contains a gerrymandering provision. Also, a few other 116th Congress bills might be worth considering for support, including Rep Jerry McNerney's *HR 2057 Fair Map Act,* Senator Michael Bennet's *S 1972 Fair Maps Act,* Rep Zoe Lofgren's *HR 3572 Redistricting Reform Act, and* Senator Amy Klobuchar's *Bill To Require Independent Redistricting*. Finally, it is also highly suggested that you go to your state on the Brennan Center gerrymandering map and review the current legislation proposed. But again, this is a particular issue you need to look deeply into, to avoid just giving undo power to one side or the other, even when they claim to be offering a "solution."

On the more technical side, there could now be a additional light at the end of the tunnel for creating a truly impartial and all-encompassing way to forever take redistricting control out of the hands of the corrupted two party system and make the process unbiased. In 2014, researchers Eric McGhee and Nick Stephanopoulos created a measurement called the efficiency gap, which calculates a numerical value for any given district showing its proportional proximity to an ideal representation of its actual populous. A company called Azavea has even used this model to generate efficiency gap numbers for all states and provide easy-to-understand explanations and infographics that describe how this mathematical model can be used to ensure future redistricting is unbiased. They even provide an amazingly slick tool for would-be activists like yourself to type in your home address and immediately get contact information on every one of your governmental representatives, from your local officials to state legislators to federal officials, so that you can email them or call them to request they begin backing an efficiency gap system.

Even if it needed to be enacted on a state-by-state basis through citizen's initiatives (Chap 9, Sec 8), creating nonpolitical redistricting commissions using the efficiency gap model as their standard for staying impartial would come the closest to solving the gerrymandering issue. This would help get America as close as possible to having ideal and accurate representation for all Americans in the legislative branch of our government, and is well worth letting your current representatives know you care about.

So, what should you do? Any or all of the following...

1) Go to Policymap.com to understand the issue of gerrymandering so you can explain it to your friends and family.

2) Go to the BrennanCenter.org to check out proposed legislation that might be worth supporting in your state.

2) Go to Azavea.com to understand the efficiency gap metric and how implementing it within independent redistricting commissions would help.

3) Go to represent.us to learn about the *American Anti-Corruption Act* and maybe sign up to help get it passed

4) Consider contacting your federal representatives (https://live.cicerodata.com) to tell them to support Brian Fitzpatrick's *CLEAN Elections Act (HR 163)*, or any and all of the other gerrymandering bills mentioned in this section.

Key Section Takeaways

Gerrymandering is the corrupt Republican and Democratic practice of redrawing congressional districts with political bias to keep themselves in power

Section B) How to Remove Partisan Gridlock from Congress

Much of the problem with our country's current system of governance comes from the above listed electoral issues, which means we're allowing the wrong people to represent us. However, even if the occasional good, honest, and independent-thinking representative gets elected, they will largely find their desire to represent their constituents completely thwarted from being bullied into party politics per usual. There are changes that need to be made to the system of legislative governance itself (Congress) to mitigate the corrupted two-party system's ability to force everyone into polarization lockstep. These following four changes to the way Congress works can easily be addressed though, and will have far-reaching impact on eliminating the two-parties' hold over our chosen representatives.

Congress B1: *Liberate the Speaker of the House from Partisanship*

Understanding why selection of the Speaker of the House should be less partisan is important, and also requires a little understanding of how the House of Representatives itself works. The Speaker of the House of Representatives is not only second in line for the presidency, behind the vice president, but is also paramount in setting the tone and function of each Congress. They are the single most important individual in the country as to which laws are actually seriously considered for becoming law. Bottom line, it would improve everything if they were above party control.

Among their many duties and powers, the Speaker of the House appoints members and chairpersons of regular committees, special or select committees, and conference committees; designates a majority of the Committee on Rules; determines which legislation is assigned to each committee and which legislation reaches the House floor for a vote; including determining the overall House legislative agenda. Without going into all of the mechanics of how a bill (proposed law) becomes a law, which you can quickly brush up on at ballotpedia.org, it is suffice for you to know that whoever is chosen to be Speaker of the House, and wherever their loyalties lie, influences to a great extent what any given Congress will actually achieve.

Unsurprisingly however, the modern Speaker of the House has sadly devolved into a position as head cheerleader for either the red or the blue team, more than having any interest in ensuring Congress functions well for the whole country, as was the position's original intent. The good thing is that there are actually few rules set in the Constitution for how the Speaker of the House is selected, so it can be changed for the better. The Constitution does not state that the Speaker must even be chosen by the House of Representatives, for instance.

The first change we should make, as the great anti-polarization group *No Labels* proposes, is requiring a 60 percent margin in the House for anyone attempting to become Speaker. Some more radical reform ideas have suggested taking the selection of the Speaker away from the House completely and giving it to some sort of independent commission or mass vote, however, simply forcing a non-polarized majority to agree on who it is would largely improve the selection without adding unnecessary complications or delays. Requiring this strong of a majority within the House of Representatives would ensure that an extremely partisan individual could not receive enough support to win, and immediately encourage more nonpartisan candidates for Speaker. It would also force communication and compromise between the two major existing parties.

As Mikey Edwards points out in the *The Parties versus the People*, "There is no requirement in the Constitution that the Speaker be a member of Congress. It is quite possible for a House member to nominate for the Speakership a respected American who does not serve in Congress." But even if always requiring only non-members of Congress for consideration of the Speakership is a bridge too far, it is still reasonable to at least expect those who achieve the Speakership to publicly renounce all party affiliation, as is comparable to the Speaker's role in both Great Britain and Canada. If it were required that no individual elected Speaker of the House could ever be endorsed by, caucus with, campaign for, or receive funds from a political party again after accepting the position, it would go a long way toward ensuring the least partisan individuals, whether from inside the House or outside it, would be selected for the position. And, if the individual selected for the Speakership categorically cannot be of benefit to, or receive benefit from any political party, it would be a huge step to immediately making the function of Congress as a whole less partisan and corrupt. It would effectively cut one of the heads off the two party beast.

Edwards continues, “We Americans have long assumed that the Speaker is, in fact, supposed to be the partisan leader of whichever party controls the House. But the Speaker could play a very different role, overseeing a completely nonpartisan division of committees, guaranteeing a nonpartisan process for considering legislation on the House floor, and serving as a mediator to push the competing parties toward common ground and effective problem solving.” This was the role originally required by the Speaker for our government to properly function, and with this minor change, we could go a long way to restoring the position’s positive use.

So, what can you do? Any or all of the following...

1) Go to nolabels.org to watch a video about The Speaker Project and sign up to lend your support.

2) Put pressure on local, state, and federal representatives through directly emailing or calling to tell them you want the role of Speaker of the House improved. Use Azavea’s technology (located at https://live.cicerodata.com), and even go to this book’s Sample Representative Letter (Appendix One) for a template.

Key Section Takeaways

The Speaker of the House is arguably the most powerful person in the country for what laws are passed

Forcing this position to be less partisan would help everything

Congress B2: *Liberate Congressional Committees from Partisan Corruption*

Between the House and the Senate there are over 250 committees and subcommittees. These committees are extremely important, as in order for any bill (proposed law) to even be considered for vote into law by all the members of either chamber it must be approved by the committee it was assigned to. If you want quick, free summaries of the way this process works go to ballotpedia.org. Suffice to say, there are approximately eight thousand bills proposed annually, and only about 10 percent of these ever make it to the floor for a vote on possibly becoming a law, the rest "dying in committee." The few members chosen by party leadership to serve on each committee then have tremendous power in determining which bills have any chance of ever becoming a law, and the process needs more scrutiny and reform.

Letting unfavored laws "die in committee" is a rampant, often unethical, and extremely powerful tactic used by both the Republicans and Democrats to subvert the will of the people. If Congress was actually working to produce the best laws for all America, many more high-quality bills would reach the floor of the House for a vote by the "portrait of the people at large." As it is, however, we end up having a completely dysfunctional and corrupt democracy, where even well-intended and popular legislation can never see the light of day for consideration due to a few strategically placed two-party system bad actors. If you want to see an explanation of how little your opinion actually matters to legislation passed, check out Represent.Us' short video, "Unbreaking America."

As former Congressman Mikey Edwards again points out, "In theory, the committees exist to deliberate about the best solutions to major national problems; in reality, they exist to advance the partisan agenda of a temporary majority—or, for members of the minority, to block that agenda…" If we are to have a functioning democracy, it cannot be overstated how vastly improved things could be by removing, or at least mitigating, partisan ideology from these committees. Luckily, this can be achieved.

For instance, instead of the majority party exercising majority control on every committee, which is now the standard, the committees could be randomly mixed with congressmen from all parties and ideologies. Congress only needs alter its own rules (just rules, not even laws) to no longer allow party leadership to pick who goes on what committees. It can even assign seats based on completely random, computerized number selection. Chairpersons for each committee could be assigned based on seniority—not party affiliation—so as to have a seasoned member of Congress overseeing the committee's work, but the rest can be filled randomly. That is, after all, what congressional representatives are supposedly there to do. Party control isn't ever mentioned in the Constitution and therefore shouldn't have any merit as a standing part of government. Of course, any members of congress should be free to associate with whomever they feel best helps them serve their constituency and the country, but not allowing artificial party divides on committees would immediately ensure that different ideologies must be heard and discussed, which is the entire point of the committees in the first place. Again, we need to start fighting against the overall brainwashing the Republicans and Democrats are doing, that their parties have some inherent place in the actual structure of our governmental system. They don't.

So, what should you do? Any or all of the following…

1) Put pressure on local, state, and federal representatives by emailing them that you want the role of congressional committees improved. This is a prime example of an issue that can be influenced by contacting your congressional representatives as they are the ones who decide these rules. Use Azavea's technology (located at https://live.cicerodata.com) to tell them that you want congressional committees to be less polarized through changing the rules of who gets assigned to them.

2) Tell anyone and everyone about this issue and solution and why it is important.

Key Section Takeaways

Congressional committees are important to understand, and fight against being partisan

Congress B3: *Restrict Incumbent Congressional Members' Fundraising Time*

On April 24, 2016, the television show *60 Minutes* ran a "Dialing for Dollars" expose of the shocking amount of time sitting congressional members spent soliciting funds for their political parties rather than doing the job of creating appropriate legislation for American citizens. By many estimates, both representatives in the House and Senate, from both the Republicans and Democrats, were spending over four hours of every work day, thirty hours each week, in party-required telemarketing rooms soliciting donations. Once fundraising dinners, parties, and personal visits were included, many estimates were up to 75 percent of these federally elected officials' time is spent trying to raise money for their affiliated party, at the expense of doing the job they were hired to do by the electorate. Seventy-five percent of their time! Three quarters of the time, the guy or gal you voted for to help you, is essentially just making deals with lobbyists and oligarch representatives to keep themselves in power and get richer. At best, and this is even probably doubtful, they are only allocating 25 percent of their time to acting, thinking, or caring about representing you and finding solutions for the good of the country.

And to be clear, this is not just Congressmen independently choosing to raise funds for their own reelections. This absurd amount of time spent asking people for money is REQUIRED by BOTH the Republican and Democratic parties, with many of those raised funds being directed back to the parties rather than the individual representative. If a representative tries to buck this system, they would most likely lose support from their two-party masters and be out of their job because of all the electoral system rigging we discussed earlier. So again, we have a situation whereby even if someone runs for and somehow gets elected to office with the best of intentions, they're not even allowed to act on them without rendering themselves politically null and void.

Almost as troubling as representatives being held at ransom to use all their time producing funds for their party is where those donations are coming from. A majority of the funds are coming from lobbyists, special interests, and other factions of our oligarchy in a blatant "money for political favors" transaction. But of course it is... who else would it be coming from? This subject will be covered in more detail in Chapter Six, but suffice to say, things need to change. For the purposes of this section of the book, it is good enough for you to just realize that the person you elected to Congress to oversee yours and the country's best interest is immediately placed in a system that forces him to sell his political soul to the highest bidder for his party, thereby enriching those entrenched at the top over all else. In modern America, this has sadly become your representative's chief priority, not representing you.

In 2015, David Jolly introduced the *Stop Act*, or HR 4443, to the 115th Congress that was a simple and direct law to forbid any federally elected officials from actively soliciting funds. Straightforward, common sense, very achievable. You can watch David Jolly summarize it to his congressional peers by searching Youtube for "David Jolly Stop Act." Naturally however, this law did not get passed by the very people it is meant to restrict, and died in committee as the 115th Congress adjourned. It does not, though, mean that this same bill, or a very similar one, can't be reintroduced if there is enough grassroots pressure by us on Congress to do it. A great example of a new bill is the *American Anti-Corruption Act* by the amazing organization Represent.Us.

Many bills that have eventually become law have had to be reintroduced to Congress several times. By you letting your Congress person know you are aware of the situation, care about it, and refuse to allow it to continue, a similar law can be passed. Or, as with there *American Anti-Corruption Act*, bills can even potentially be passed on the local and state levels that effectively bypass a corrupt Congress and beat them at their own games.

So, what can you do. Any or all of the following...

1) Put pressure on local, state, and federal representatives to stop spending a majority of their time raising funds for their party. Thanks to Azavea's technology (located at https://live.cicerodata.com), you can literally find the phone numbers and emails of your representatives for free within about five seconds. Tell them that you want a law passed similar to the *Stop Act HR 4443* from the 115th Congress, which would restrict or forbid sitting congressional members from fundraising.

2) Go to Represent.Us and learn about the *American Anti-Corruption Act* and lend your efforts to help it become law in your area.

Key Section Takeaways

Your congressional representative is not thinking about your well-being right now. They're trying to get wealthy people to give them money in exchange for favorable legislation, and that should make you mad. Chapter 6 has even more information about money's role in politics.

Congress B4: ***Support the "Fulcrum Strategy" at UniteAmerica, the "Problem Solvers" from No Labels, and the "Reformers Caucus" from Issue One***

UniteAmerica.org, NoLabels.org, and IssueOne.org have independently both come up very creative strategies for influencing American politics back toward a more moderate, nonpartisan center. Supporting all, or any, would definitely help things.

The core of *Unite America's* effort is the "fulcrum strategy," offering a quick and powerful blow to the two-party system without changing any existing rules or laws. In the US Senate, and around twenty-four state legislatures, most legislative majorities are only separated by three to five individuals. What *Unite America* proposes to do with the fulcrum strategy is actively recruit moderates and independents into these legislative bodies so as to populate each of them with a winning "swing vote" coalition block. These moderate legislators would have already renounced loyalty to either of the main two parties and would instead promise to work to create moderation, compromise, and solutions within any legislative votes. The impact in some of these legislative bodies could be hugely powerful, effectively ending either wing of the two-party's control, and at a minimum would force them to at least consider moderate and bipartisan solutions to any issues. You can go to uniteamerica.org to read more details about the fulcrum strategy and watch a quick video explaining the concept.

In an entirely different effort, but with a similar long term goal, *No Labels* has created a *Problem Solvers* Caucus that is re-training Congressmen on how to work across the aisle to achieve bi-partisan results. And, since 2018, they are actually getting results. You can go to nolables.org to learn more about the Problem Solvers caucus, but just like with the fulcrum strategy, the main thing to know is that you should try to get your representatives to participate in it.

Last, but not least, *Issue One* has created a growing non-partisan movement of past governmental officials and grassroots participants called the "Reformers Caucus," which primarily aims to increase one-person one-vote democracy through lessening big money's impact, and restoring ethical standards to government.

So, what can you do? Any or all of the following...

1) Go to uniteamerica.org to learn more about their platform and the "fulcrum strategy," and sign up

2) Do the same at nolables.org, learning about their "Problem Solvers Caucus"

3) Check out IssueOne.org and maybe sign up to participate

2) Put pressure on local, state, and federal representatives through directly emailing or calling to tell them you want them to join *UniteAmerica's, IssueOne's,* and *NoLabel's* platforms. Thanks to Azavea's technology (located at https://live.cicerodata.com), you can literally find the phone numbers and emails of your representatives for free within about five seconds.

Key Section Takeaways

There are some groups like No Labels and Unite America that have some great ideas on how to make politics less partisan. You should demand your representatives participate.

Congress B5: *Enact Term Limits on Congress*

Fun question... what do Donald Trump, Barack Obama, and about 80 percent of all Americans regardless of race, gender, age, or ideology agree on? Requiring term limits for congressional representatives and senators! Second fun question: then why has a congressional term limit law never been passed by lawmakers, despite multiple bills being submitted addressing the issue? You actually already know the answer to this one... because, much like sterner laws against lobbying money flowing to them, it's going to take some effort to force Congress to pass legislation to limit how long they can stay in Washington getting rich.

Currently, senators and House representatives can legally get re-elected indefinitely without restriction. Unlike presidents or most governors, who are limited to a total of eight years, members of Congress often end up serving multiple terms with some even staying in office for the vast majority of their lifetimes, even over fifty years. This is a far cry from the "citizen-statesmen" our founding fathers envisioned making up each Congress, whereby normal Americans with nonpolitical careers would take brief stints to Washington to represent their neighbors in government. What we now have is a modern scourge of career politicians who go to Washington and never leave, vastly increasing their own wealth and power through the systemic two-party corruption they ensure. A lack of term limits on Congress was even considered by Thomas Jefferson to be the greatest flaw of the Constitution.

Term limits are a clear-cut and simple way to reduce the power of the two parties while ensuring fresh voices and ideas get continually circulated into the legislative branch. It would also go a long ways toward eliminating lobbying-based corruption. People arguing against term limits for Congress are normally somehow benefiting from Washington corruption themselves, or just don't really understand their importance. These opponents of congressional term limits typical rely on just a few very thin points.

First, they will sometimes claim that Congressmen and women provide the only real check to presidential power, so to force them out of office based on some arbitrary timeframe potentially shifts more control to the executive branch. Not true. Most congressional representatives are doing nothing to check the presidency now, so why are those same exact individual crucial to doing it in the future? Besides, many congressional term limit proposals will give senators and representatives an entire twelve years before their limit in office is up, which is still fifty percent longer than any president is allowed to serve. Keeping the presidency in check is extremely important, but it is up to the legislative and judicial branches as a whole, not some supposed individual congress person that needs more than a decade to get warmed up. Restoring the full power of the legislative branch will come to fruition much quicker with an entire nonpartisan overhaul, rather than keeping those already corrupted free to stay forever.

Second, some people claim we "already have term limits" called elections, and if a congressman or woman is not doing a good job they can be voted out. Again, weak argument. As we've already discussed in the above sections, any incumbent Congressman is at a huge advantage as long as he stays loyal to his party masters, so much so that it is debatable if we can even claim to still have free and meaningful elections. Once the two main parties have chosen their lackeys to install in Congress, it is virtually impossible to get rid of them without term limits. Granted, the changes listed in other sections above will rectify a lot of issues, but term limits would serve as an extremely powerful check against the lobbying, career-politician, thinking that has infected DC for decades.

Last, some people will claim it is a bad idea to force a great senator or representative to quit on a preordained timeframe if they are doing an amazing job, as the good ones will only achieve more the longer they stay. This argument seems to speak more to how bad our overall system has become than anything else. Do we really want to give unlimited power to someone because they happen to be one of the few people doing a good job? Or should we maybe correct the system so that there is accountability for most people to do a good job, and an abundance of good people serving the will of the people in government? We've got over 300 million people to choose from, after all.

George Washington was arguably America's greatest leader and he willingly stepped down after two terms to allow fresh thinking. American history has been filled with brilliant politicians and courageous leaders, but at no point did they serve lifetime appointments in one role. In fact, it could be argued that the concept of any elected official holding the same position for any length of time spanning decades is un-American. America was founded on the principle of diversification of power, as it was a clear alternative to "king-like" power that the founding fathers intentionally broke from. Allowing a congressional representative to stay in power indefinitely does not increase their ability to get things done, but makes them more susceptible to the same inherent dangers of laziness, disconnection, and corruption of every monarch, despot, and lifetime appointee that has come before them. Mr. and Mrs. Congressional Representative, we truly appreciate the time you've spent pretending to protect the people's will in government—now don't let the door hit you in the ass on your way out as you get back to bartending, mowing lawns, or selling insurance like the rest of us.

In this area, a few Republicans have actually been taking the forefront to get legislation passed. One of them is Senator Ted Cruz, who at the start of the 116th Congress, again introduced a constitutional amendment (*SJ Res 1*)to impose term limits of eighteen years on members of Congress. As mentioned above, without strong and incessant grassroots pressure from you, us, and everyone on our current representatives to pass this, the proposal will probably languish without action as has always happened previously. There are also a couple of other Republicans, Representative Brian Fitzpatrick and Representative Norman of South Carolina, who have introduced their own term limit bills in *HJ Res 12* and *HR 198 VOICE Act*. Passing any of these appear to be a step in the right direction.

An additional effort for finally getting congressional term limits comes from a group called, conveniently enough, US Term Limits (termlimits.com). USTL is leading a rapidly growing grassroots effort to invoke an Article 5 constitutional amendment permanently installing limits on how long any congressman or woman can stay in office. Article 5 is the process for overcoming Congress' reluctance to regulate itself, going through the states to initiate an appropriate constitutional amendment. Obviously, getting an amendment through the Article 5 process requires a lot of coordination and communication, which is why it is extremely effective to give your support to this already existing and well-organized group. And actually, the quickest way we can be sure to get much needed term limits is for you to simultaneously support all these efforts and any others you can find.

So, what should you do? Any or all of the following...

1) Go to termlimits.com and sign their petition, enroll for updates, read more about the issue and solution, donate, and lend your support.

2) Put pressure on local, state, and federal representatives through emailing or calling to tell them you want them to support Senator Cruz's proposed constitutional amendment (*SJ Res 1*), and/ or Rep Fitzpatrick's *HJ Res 12*, and/or Rep Norman's

The VOICE Act. (find them at https://live.cicerodata.com)

Key Section Takeaways

Pretty much everything would be improved if we forced Congress to have term limits the same way we do for the President

Additional Actions for All Chapter Four Issues

In addition to the more specific sections suggestions listed in the proceeding chapter there are always three helpful general actions you can take at any time (below). It's also suggested to go to Appendix Three to check out additional bills in the current Congress that might be relevant to an issue.

1) Continue putting pressure on local, state, and federal representatives through directly emailing or calling to tell them stating you want one issue, or multiple ones, fixed. With Azavea's technology (located at https://live.cicerodata.com), you can quickly find the phone numbers and emails of everyone who represents you in all forms of government for free. You can even use this book's Sample Representative Letter (Appendix One) as an email template for sending to them.

2) If you are more ambitious to be a leader in reform, go to Change.org to start a petition (or a citizen's initiative if your state allows) for addressing the issue. A citizen's initiative is a petition that formally forces a legislative body to convene and vote on an issue (see Chap 9, Sec 8). Each state has its own rules and processes for starting a citizen's initiative, but regardless, you can get the ball rolling by easily starting a petition at change.org. Their system even helps you send your petition out to all your social media contacts.

3) Tell anyone and everyone about these issues and why they're important. This step is much more important than you might think, as the grassroots sharing of ideas is where all real change first happens. Or, simply give them this book or direct them to the other listed resources for more information. And sign up at independ.me for future updates, as well as subscribe to the "Independ Me" youtube channel.

Chapter Five

Freeing Our Presidency from Polarization and Corruption

Due to their executive role over the world's largest economy, access to its greatest technological advances, and leadership of the deadliest military on the globe, every newly elected president of the United States is literally, and immediately, the most powerful person in the history of the earth. And every presidential election cycle we've come to expect "get out the vote" campaigns which use celebrities trying to convince you that your vote really, really matters as to who this person ends up being. Well, we hate to tell you this, but it's doesn't. In our current system the election of president is extremely important, yet your individual vote really, really doesn't matter for who it ends up being. No, stop whining, it just doesn't.

For instance, did you know that in our current system:

- A candidate can become president by winning only eleven states, while the majority of citizens in all the other 41 states vote against them.

- A candidate can even win the presidency with as little as only 23 percent of American citizens voting for them and everyone else (77 percent of the country) voting against them.

- The Electoral College skews people's votes for president so much that a single vote from someone from Wyoming (less populous) carries around 3.6 times more weight than one from California (more populous).

- Because of closed primaries, fraudulent debate rules, and biased campaign finance laws, the odds are astronomically small that you will ever even be able to vote for anyone with a reasonable chance of winning the presidency other than those "lesser of two evils" who the Republican and Democratic power brokers have already selected for you.

Now, before you start angrily accusing this book of fighting for voter apathy just because we're pointing out that your vote currently doesn't really matter, it is actually our radical position for you to do something much more important than just a kabuki theater "rock the vote" once every four years... why don't you change the system so that your vote for the critically important job of president does count! All you need to do is:

A) Fight for a few changes so that you can actually elect who you want for the job of president (electoral reform).

And...

B) Fight to make sure the president actually does what they are supposed to do once you give them the job (governing reform).

Section A) How to Make Presidential Elections More Fair

President A1: *Break the Electoral College*

Chief among changes to our system of electing presidents is to finally do away with the Electoral College. Whether or not the electoral college should exist is another one of those illogically polarizing arguments by the way, with the left typically being in favor of removing it and the right insisting it must stay. In this case, the left is right. Doing away with, or at least reforming, the electoral college would strengthen the one person, one vote democracy we need. End of story.

The Electoral College was originally created to bolster the idea of a constitutional republic by making sure all states, even the least populous, had some real influence on who became president. Much of this book supports Americans' understanding of a republic and fighting for reestablishing states' rights where appropriate. However, in this instance, it is well past time for the Electoral College to come to an end. If you'd like a succinct explanation of ten problems with the Electoral College, read Eric Black's 2012 article in the *MinnPost*. Suffice to say, the president is essentially the only elected federal office to represent ALL Americans, as opposed to being tied to a specific geographic region (like district or state), and therefore, should be elected by ALL Americans equally. How does that not make sense?

The Electoral College currently does not mathematically reflect the will of a majority of Americans through its winner-take-all system, or even weigh all Americans' votes equally, but is primed for manipulation by the two-party system. Most people don't realize when you cast your vote on election day you are not actually even voting for the actual presidential candidate, but choosing a handful of electoral college voters selected by the Republican and Democratic parties, who then get together a month later and pick the president. In many states, these electoral voters are not even legally required to vote based on their state's popular vote tally, providing yet another layer of disconnect between you and the end result, with a handful of powerful Republicans and Democrats largely pulling those in-between strings. The bottom line is that the Electoral College is a poor system to reflect the will of a majority of America citizens for any given vote, and even when it gets lucky and does so, there is still a robust chance of manipulation by the Republicans and Democrats.

Removing the Electoral College would not only be immediately more democratic, but would also help facilitate independents and third parties having a viable chance of winning. Additionally, removing the Electoral College would do away with the incredibly skewed "battleground state" campaigning that now occurs where candidates for the office largely ignore concerns for states outside of those few that can tip the Electoral College vote in their favor. Campaigning and governing with preferential focus on electoral college battleground states is a large problem. As explained in this quote from the *National Popular Vote* movement: "State winner-take-all statutes adversely affect governance. 'Battleground' states receive 7% more federal grants than 'spectator' states, twice as many presidential disaster declarations, more Superfund enforcement exemptions, and more No Child Left Behind law exemptions." That's crazy—the Electoral College does not let certain people's votes count based on geography, and those same states even get treated shittier by the federal government for the next four years!

Removing the Electoral College would positively alter presidential campaigning, platform concerns, and even federal governance to be more inclusive of the entire country. It would also help ensure all Americans' votes counted equally no matter where they lived, which is the core principle of our democracy. Luckily, as with financial reform, the Electoral College issue has garnered enough national attention to spawn a myriad of different groups attempting to change things. This, however, also creates a need to focus on a few of the better specific movements, to increase the odds of getting results.

As of the time of this book's publishing, there were currently three separate proposals (Cohen, Schatz, Merkley) for constitutional amendments abolishing the electoral college in the 116th Congress. If passed, any of these amendment to the Constitution would permanently do away with the electoral college and force future presidential elections to be decided by a simple popular vote. As this is the cleanest and most lasting way to do away with the Electoral College, it is well worth contacting your representatives and demanding they support the effort. Getting one of these amendments to the Constitution will require passing both houses by a two-thirds majority though, and then being ratified by thirty-eight states. In today's political climate that will be extremely hard and take a long time, so it is probably a good idea to explore other solutions concurrently.

One group worth supporting is *Equal Citizens*, which is attempting to achieve several reforms, a primary one stopping the "winner-take-all" portion of electoral voting through filing lawsuits against individual states. The state-sanctioned, winner-take-all portion of the electoral system is arguably the core problem, so winning state lawsuits to stop it is a viable strategy, even while supporting the more definitive constitutional change to develop. You can simply go to their website to sign up (equalcitizens.us).

Another, even more unique, and potentially quicker, avenue to concurrently pursue is through the *National Popular Vote* (www.nationalpopularvote.com) movement. They are generating a lot of momentum toward a unique idea of getting enough states to agree to an "interstate compact" to award the presidency through the Electoral College to whoever wins the popular vote. This will essentially render the worst attributes of the Electoral College moot, even if it technically still exists for a while. As their website describes, “The National Popular Vote interstate compact would not take effect until enacted by states possessing a majority of the electoral votes—that is, enough to elect a President (270 of 538). Under the compact, the national popular vote winner would be the candidate who received the most popular votes from all 50 states (and DC) on Election Day. When the Electoral College meets in mid-December, the national popular vote winner would receive all of the electoral votes of the enacting states.”

So what can you do? Any and all of the following...

1) Go to equalcitizens.us to sign up and maybe donate, helping support their state lawsuits overturning the “winner-take-all” portion of the Electoral College.

2) Go to nationalpopularvote.com to join the fight and spread the word regarding getting states on board with their interstate compact.

3) Tell all your governmental representatives that you are tired of the Electoral College and want them to support any or all of the three constitutional amendments proposed (Cohen HJ Res 7, Schatz SJ Res 17, Merkley SJ Res 16) to abolish it. With Azavea’s technology (located at https://live.cicerodata.com), you can find the phone numbers and emails of your representatives for free within about five seconds.

Key Section Takeaways

The electoral college is outdated, and abolishing it would strengthen our one-person, one-vote, democracy

President A2: *Make a Fair, Nationwide Primary System for the Presidential Election*

Again, states' rights and the idea of a republic are incredibly important to the proper functioning of our democracy, but specifically in regards to electing the nationwide office of president they have become outdated and counterproductive. Our current presidential primary system has two major issues with it:

1. Many states still allow closed primaries for the two parties already in power.

2. Even if all states had open primaries, due to the haphazard timing of each state's individual primary, there would still be the problem of "front-loading." Front-loading is the term describing states holding their primaries earlier (like New Hampshire and Iowa) to get outsized political attention relative to their population, thus reinforcing that some people's choice in later voting states might not even matter. Once it is their time to vote in later primaries, the presidential candidate has already effectively been selected.

As already mentioned in the prior congressional chapter, closed primaries do nothing except ensure the most extreme candidates of each party are your only choices in the general election, as it is the most extreme, partisan individuals who are choosing them. Closed primaries are a non-constitutionally sanctioned, carefully orchestrated, Republican and Democratic bulwark against anyone except red or blue diehards ever being options for the more reasonable middle of the country. Closed primaries are a major reason behind there being fewer and fewer moderates to pick from for president. On top of that, the delegate, super-delegate, and caucus systems once again ensure there is less direct accountability of elections to individual voters, and even more room for corrupt shenanigans as to who gets presented as one of your few choices come election day. Please go to Chapter Four and read Section A2 on changing closed primaries to open primaries if you'd like even more information.

In regards to the issue of front-loading presidential primaries, there are several reform plans already proposed, with one of the most promising being called the Graduated Random Presidential Primary System, or simply the American Plan. You can go to Wikipedia "Graduated Random Presidential Primary" to get a more detailed explanation of the American Plan, but the gist is that it would structure and coordinate all primaries around the country so that there are fairer processes in regards to timing. States would be required to hold presidential primaries in staggered, randomly rotating geographical blocks to ensure that no particular states ever got to dominate the process, and thus ensure that presidential campaign attention would over time be evenly distributed across the country. FairVote.org is an endorser of this plan.

Additionally, the nonprofit organization OpenPrimaries.org is fighting on both the federal and state levels to create open primaries across the country. They continue to support efforts to get legislation similar to the *Open Our Democracy (H.R. 2981)* bill of the 115th Congress voted into law to end closed primaries and gerrymandering. You should definitely consider looking into and supporting all of these efforts.

So what should you do? Any or all of the following...

1) Go to OpenPrimaries.org to watch a video explaining why closed primaries are bad, as well as give your support to bringing open primaries to every state in the country. You can also even send an email of support for the *Open Our Democracy (H.R. 2981)* bill directly to your representative with this convenient form openprimaries.org/open-our-democracy-2017

2) Sign up at FairVote.org to support the American Plan and many other positive reforms.

3) Raise this issue to your friends and family, and either give them a copy of this book or direct them to the provided resources to learn more.

Key Section Takeaways

We need a coordinated national primary so that voting for President can be fair to all Americans

President A3: ***Install Ranked-Choice Voting (aka Instant Runoff Elections) for President***

In 2016 Donald Trump won the presidency with only a vote of around 20 percent of all Americans. That means 80 percent of Americans voted for someone else, or didn't feel it was worthwhile to vote for anyone, regarding the most powerful job in the world. Leaving all curse words out of this sentence, the fact that someone can become president with only one out of five Americans wanting them to is simply not an ideal stat for the world's greatest democracy.

Part of our problem is that our current system of voting for president is a "pluralistic" one, as opposed to a majority. In a pluralistic system no candidate has to convince a majority of Americans to vote for them, only the most voters of any bracketed demographic. This once again tends to favor extremist candidates who can easily motivate smaller voting blocks, and is certainly adding to the polarization of our country. Paul Raebern's *Newsweek* article explains how the 2106 election could have been conducted in a manner more representative of true democracy through ranked-choice voting. Kevin Zollman, a game theorist and associate professor of philosophy at Carnegie Mellon University, is quoted in the article as saying, "Everybody has their favorite version of voting, but it's fair to say that almost everybody agrees that the current way we do it is the worst. The big problem with the way we do elections now is we don't ask people for their second choice."

What Raebern and the article go on to explain is how ranked-choice voting (also known as instant runoff elections) would quickly improve the way we select our president. The basics are this: when you vote for president you would pick your top choice, then rank the rest of the candidates according to who you'd pick second, third, and even fourth. If no candidate receives more than 50 percent of the eligible first-place votes, the lowest first-place vote getter would be eliminated. Since that lowest candidate has been eliminated, anyone who gave them their first-place vote now has their second choice bumped up to first, in turn changing all the vote totals. This re-tallying of the votes possibly gives someone an actual 50 percent majority to win the presidency, ensuring that the winner is at least the first or second choice for most Americans. If the first round does not produce a majority winner however, then the next lowest first-place vote getter is also eliminated. Once again, all the second-choice picks behind him are added as first-place votes to the tallies of the remaining contenders. Eventually, someone must mathematically receive a majority of the eligible votes by at least being most people's second or third choice, not their absolute last. This system ensures that the most aggregately favorable candidate for all Americans is eventually selected, rather than letting the last choice of most Americans win because of a highly motivated minority. This is a much preferable system for breaking the two party's hold over American politics, as it essentially removes the "wasted vote" argument that many red and blue sycophants try to bully independents with in every election cycle. If you find this written explanation cumbersome to grasp, just head to fairvote.org to watch a great free video with visual explanations.

As Greg Orman wrote for *Real Clear Politics*, "In a ranked-choice election, the only way to waste your vote is to actually vote against a candidate. As long as the candidate you like least doesn't reach the 50 percent threshold, they won't win. So only positive votes matter... Ranked-choice voting effectively allows voters to vote their actual preferences instead of having to vote strategically. This would have a meaningful impact on elections and governing. It would empower independent and third party candidates by eliminating the 'wasted vote' argument."

Granted, ranked-choice voting would function way

better for president if we also did away with the Electoral College and closed primaries, but it would alone be a vast improvement and immediately do more for giving independent candidates a real chance at the White House than anything else. As is shown in a list on FairVote.org, ranked-choice voting is already being used with great success in multiple state and local elections around the country. Maine has already instituted legislation to change all elections (municipal, state, and congressional) except presidential to ranked-choice voting. The only real hang up with ranked-choice voting being implemented for president at this point is simply in explaining the concept to the nation as a whole and thereby putting pressure on officials to institute it.

Getting ranked-choice voting for president can be tackled through congressional and state-based actions and will be an extremely powerful change in the right direction. Luckily, an organization, aptly called Ranked Choice Voting, is helping to provide resources for any activists fighting for the change, including an incredible free webinar series you can watch to wrap your head around the idea and be able to explain to your friends and family why naysayers are wrong. The Center for Election Science is also trying to help any geographic areas that desire moving toward more fair, logical, and representative voting systems. Either of these organizations, along with the always on point FairVote.org, could use your support regarding this issue.

So what can you do? Any or all of the following...

1) Sign up at rankedchoicevoting.org to learn more about the solution, lend your support, spread the word on why moving to ranked-choice voting systems around the country would improve our democracy and lessen our polarization.

2) Sign up at FairVote.org to back their powerful

movements for election reform

3) Sign up at The Center for Election Sciences as well to learn more about why ranked choice voting is better. (electology.org)

4) Go to represent.us to learn about the American Anti-Corruption Act and maybe support getting it passed in your community.

Key Section Takeaways

Ranked choice voting is a better way to vote for anything and everything, and we should be using it in all our elections.

President A4: *Reform the Rules Regarding Televised Presidential Debates*

At first glance this might seem trivial, but it is indeed not. Although decreasing slightly since the advent of the internet, the televised presidential debates are arguably still the most impactful event for most Americans to form their voting opinion around. Unfortunately, like with many other areas we're covering in this book, since the 1980s the Republicans and Democrats have successfully gamed this to give themselves preferential treatment, prevent third-party and independent candidates from participating, and ensure the process is easy as possible for themselves. The debates offer a powerful opportunity for the country to compare candidate intelligence, character, and temperament within a pressured and unscripted environment, but we must reform both their selection process and formats to return them to legitimacy. Until third-party candidates are allowed into the televised debates, the reality is that most Americans will not think any are worthy of voting for —and the entrenched Republicans and Democrats know this.

Since 1987, the *Commission for Presidential Debates* has been the entity that oversees the format and frequency for how candidates will compete within the debates as well as, most importantly of all, who is allowed to participate. When being created, this commission was billed as being a nonpartisan entity that would ensure the efficiency and fairness of presidential debates, but as with most things that the two-party system has sneakily gained control over, the privately run commission is anything but nonpartisan and fair. The *Commission on Presidential Debates* has been entirely staffed by extreme Republican and Democratic party loyalists since its inception. They consistently, and completely, keep out any independent candidates besides their chosen two through use of their sham "polling" system for qualification. Their rule requires any candidate to poll at 15 percent across the nation before the debates in a compilation of polls solely selected by the commission. This is an artificially high number for any candidate not relying on the structure of the Republicans and Democrats to achieve seven weeks before the election.

Unfortunately, this almost certain exclusion from the debates then reinforces that qualified people, who do not wish to kowtow to the Republicans or Democrats, can't viably consider running. It then also discourages anyone from potentially funding these independent campaigns, since everyone knows a nationwide audience cannot be obtained. Two-party sycophants will argue that we need to keep "unqualified" candidates from wasting Americans' time within the debates, but like with everything else regarding our current rigged system, this is a large manipulation of a very small real concern in order to protect Republicans and Democrats. It is actually extremely straightforward and easy to change presidential debates so that only the most likely few candidates to win are included, yet not requiring all of those candidates to necessarily have a red or blue tie on for participation. Those currently winning the game simply want to keep things as easy for themselves as possible, and not run the risk of being shown up on national television by any real competition.

Change the Rule and *Level the Playing Field* are two groups leading the way on "un-rigging" the presidential debates. C*hange the Rule* is fighting for an overhaul of how non-Republican and Democrat candidates can fairly qualify for the debates through forcing the *Commission on Presidential Debates* to revise its qualification rule. From their website: "We propose an additional rule that we think is a far better indicator of national support and demonstrates the grassroots organization necessary to mount a legitimate presidential bid – a ballot access signature competition. The new rule would work as follows: On April 30 any candidate, party, or nominating process with ballot access in states that collectively have at least 270 Electoral College votes would notify the CPD of that access.

If there is more than one, then whoever has gathered the most signatures as part of the ballot access process will participate in the debates with the Democratic and Republican nominees. Under this new rule, for the first time in our history, an independent candidate can be designated to be in the debates at least six months before the election." This is a much fairer and more reasonable process for determining who will be in the debates and would make it more difficult for any overseeing entity to manipulate. It is also very easy to quickly change. As it is simply regarding one rule written by the few individuals making up the commission, they could effectively rewrite it tomorrow. Pressure, with your help, is just needed to make them do it.

Level the Playing Field is suing the *Federal Election Commission* to have them abolish, or at least properly regulate, the *Commission on Presidential Debates*. Check out Melissa Cruz's 2017 Real Clear Politics article for a summary of the current court battles. If the commission does not take it upon themselves to change, this could be a much more powerful and lasting way to change things. As James Glassman is quoted in the above article, "When you get down to it, we have a broken system that is getting more broken by the minute. It's because when we only have two parties, each one goes into its own corner. You frequently end up with extremism, while the vast majority of Americans are in the middle. Even if the independent choice doesn't win, that person would have a big impact on pulling the other candidates to the middle to create a more constructive election."

It might be best to simply do away with the Commission on Presidential Debates and create a new, truly independent commission comprised of people who have renounced party affiliation. However it is done, the idea of reforming the *Commission on Presidential Debates*, and their partisan rules, is crucial to expanding America's choice for president to new people and voices, and it will not be hard to do if we Americans stand up and demand it. Further, any regulatory body overseeing the debates should move into the twenty-first century by enhancing its ability to benefit the electorate and create accessibility for all voters.

The University of Pennsylvania's *Annenberg Public Policy Center* has also done an extensive study resulting in a "Democratizing the Debates Summary" of proposed formatting changes for the presidential debates to maximize their benefit and make them accessible for all voters. You can check out a summary of their findings at annenbergpublicpolicycenter.org/feature/democratizing-the-debates.

With the Trump-Clinton debates in 2016 breaking all-time viewership numbers of over 80 million Americans tuning in, and the country consistently inching toward further polarization, it becomes more and more important to force the televised debates into a moderate, substantive, and inclusive format, giving qualified independents and third parties an equal chance at making their case to the country-at-large. Properly reforming our televised debates would be a hugely impactful blow against polarization in the country that would not require much effort or red tape to battle through.

So what should you do? Any or all of the following...

1) Go to *Change the Rule* (changetherule.org) and sign up to stay informed and spread the word.

2) Take a look at the *Annenberg Public Policy Center* report on reforming the format of the debates, and speak to your friends and family about why it is important to both reform the debate formats along with who gets to participate. Or, just hand them this book.

3) Go to Change.org to start a petition for abolishing or reforming the Commission on Presidential Debates

4) Contract all your representatives (https://live.cicerodata.com**) and tell them that you want them to create a law to make the Presidential Debates more inclusive of independents.**

Key Section Takeaways

The Republicans and Democrats are currently rigging the televised presidential debates to keep out independents, and we need to stop them.

Section B) How to Help the Job of President Function Properly

As mentioned earlier, each and every successive president of the United States immediately becomes the most powerful person in the history of the world. As of 2018, the president was CEO of the earth's largest economy at $20 trillion, with its daily ripples affecting the livelihood of nearly everyone across the globe through the US-dominated financial system. The job also entails being commander of the world's most powerful military, including having the unchecked ability to personally blow the planet up multiple times over through roughly 6500 nuclear warheads. And, he or she is also the primary orator and architect of collective ideals for an aggregate 330 million Americans, setting the tone and message of what America, and arguably even the world, will believe is right, important, or at least inevitable. It is crucial that we not only elect the right person to the job, but that the job functions correctly once that person is in office.

By "functions correctly," this book means freeing the president to work without hinderance in their constitutionally dictated duties, yet also restricting the presidency back to only its original constitutionally designed powers in case a less-than-ideal person obtains the job. This requires knowing exactly what the role of the president was envisioned to be.

According to Article II of the Constitution the president's exclusive powers are to:

- Serve as commander in chief of the armed forces
- Commission officers of the armed forces
- Grant reprieves and pardons for federal offenses (except impeachment)
- Convene Congress in special sessions
- Receive ambassadors

- Take care that the laws be faithfully executed
- Wield the "executive power"
- Appoint officials to lesser offices

There are also additional powers that the president shares with Congress, including:

- Make treaties
- Appoint ambassadors, judges, and high officials
- Approve legislation

But that's it—they are not a king or queen with unlimited power. And it's already a lot of responsibility, more than enough for one person to do well. Obviously, there's some gray area in how you interpret the meaning of these sparse statements, but our entire government only works the way it's supposed to, when the presidency works the way it is supposed to. Over the decades the powers and expectations of the presidency have slowly shifted, however, in some ways becoming impotent to two-party-dictated gridlock, while in others becoming dangerously too powerful. It is vitally important to the successful function of our government, and therefore to the happiness, well-being, and moderate temperance of our country-at-large, to reform the job of president to be more appropriate again.

And here's how we do that...

President B1: *Return War Powers to Congress*

Article I, Section 8 of the Constitution (War Powers Clause) gives Congress the sole power to declare any and all wars—not the president. The founding fathers expressly designed our government to only commit our sons, daughters, and precious resources to the danger of battle if the collective people—through a majority of their representatives in Congress —considered a war necessary. The president's role is to be limited to commander-in-chief, overseeing the execution of the war, only once declared by Congress. He is not supposed to be the only man in the country able to choose whether or not to start one, like a king.

James Madison explained, "*The constitution supposes, what the History of all Governments demonstrates, that the Executive is the branch of power most interested in war, and most prone to it. It has accordingly with studied care vested the question of war to the Legislature.*"

Yet despite this intentional structuring of our government to give Congress the sole ability to start a war, America has had at least twelve major military conflicts, killed tens of millions of humans worldwide, and spent trillions of dollars on major military and covert operations, since the last time Congress actually declared war for World War II in 1945. Currently, America is at war with troops and/or using lethal drones and other combat technology in at least seven (probably more) different countries. And this is not to even necessarily endorse a dovish stance that all of these conflicts are necessarily bad, some may certainly be justified to protect national security in this age of terrorism, but only to point out the core problem that one man or woman should not be the sole individual making these deadly decisions with hardly any accountability, oversight, or repercussions.

As we've already acknowledged, the Constitution can

sometimes be a bit vague for the complexities of the modern world, and it is an extremely valid concern that the role of president should be able to respond to military threats quickly without having to first convene a vote in Congress. In this age of biological and nuclear weapons, our national security depends on it. However, since Congress passed the *War Powers Act* in the 1970s, it's widely accepted that these presidential actions should only be allowed on a short-term basis.

The *War Powers Act* of 1973 intelligently set up a framework of how and when a president could react quickly to a military threat versus when the president must inform and/or receive consent from Congress. It may not have been perfect, but it was at least a step in the right direction. Unfortunately, Congress has moved further and further toward completely doing away with its own constitutional responsibility to oversee decisions to go to war, by repeatedly passing more and more expansive authorization to use military force (AUMF) legislation allowing the president to do as they please and completely disregard the *War Powers Act* and the *War Powers Clause* of the Constitution. If you'd like an easy way to digest the issue, give episode 117 of the brilliant Jen Briney's *Congressional Dish* podcast a listen.

Worst of all, is that new AUMFs like S.J. Res 59, introduced in 2018 to the 115th Congress by senators Kaine and Corker, would give the president even more latitude in waging war. As Senator Rand Paul has written, this needs be stopped. Senator Paul has made valiant efforts to fix this repeated AUMF-issuing problem, but thus far has been shut down by his colleagues. It is important this issue be addressed properly by stopping the more expansive AUMF legislation, requiring time limits on any AUMF legislation that passes and demanding an adherence to the requirements in the existing War Powers Act of 1973 and the War Powers Clause of the Constitution. In the 116th Congress, Rep James Himes has introduced *HR 1193 Reclamation of War Powers Act* to help address these issues, as well as Rep Peter DeFazio putting forth the *War Powers Amendments Act HJ Res 66*.

Whether through the lens of saving lives, money, or preventing a major travesty before it occurs, the decision to use the violence of the greatest military the world has ever known should be deliberated and debated among the several, not exclusively dictated by the whims of one. True, in this day and age of deadly fast technology and borderless, irrational terrorism, it does make some sense to give the president latitude to quickly react to grave and immediate threats to our country, but those must be defined, justified, and if found to have not been warranted through examination and oversight, corrected. Restoring the president's role to a Constitutional norm would not only help government's overall function, but less two-party dysfunction, and thereby help diminish American polarization.

So, what can you do? Any and all of the following...

1) Listen to the great Jen Briney's podcast episode 117 on *Congressional Dish* where she breaks down how scary these AUMFs actually are, then speak to your friends and family on why it is so important.

2) Contact all your representatives to let them know that you want them to support *HR 1193 Reclamation of War Powers Act* and/or the *HJ Res 66 War Powers Amendment Act*, as well as fight against the passage of future AUMF like *S.J. Res 59* from the 115th Congress.

Key Section Takeaways

Congress is supposed to vote on whether or not we go to war, not just the president deciding by himself

President B2: *Require the President to Appear Before Congress to Answer Questions*

This brilliantly simple idea is taken directly from the 2016 No Labels Policy Playbook. Britain requires the prime minister to make regular visits to Parliament to publicly debate pressing issues of the day. America rarely, if ever, gets to see direct debates between our political leaders outside of election cycles. Requiring the president to make twice yearly visits to Congress to publicly defend and argue for their proposed policies would do a great deal to inform the public on government's inner workings. It would not only force the president to be more accountable to Congress and the public in his rationale but would help expose exactly what stances various members of Congress had on specific issues. If anything like Britain's process, it would also be damned entertaining.

Here's how No Labels suggest it be done: "...on a rotating basis the House and Senate would issue monthly invitations to the president to appear in the respective chamber for questions and discussion. Each question period would last 90 minutes and would be televised. The majority and minority would alternate questions. The president could, at his or her discretion, bring one or more cabinet members to the question period and refer specific questions to them."

So, what can you do? Any or all of the following...

1) Go to nolabels.org and read the "No Labels Policy Playbook" then speak to your friends and family on why this is a great idea. Or, just hand them this book.

2) Contact all your representatives to let them know that you want them to propose the idea of the

president being required to appear before them to answer questions. Located at https://live.cicerodata.com, you can literally find the phone numbers and emails of your representatives for free within about five seconds. Even use this book's Sample Representative Letter to see and/or use an email template for sending to them.

Key Section Takeaways

We should think outside the box, and do stuff like require the President to publicly account for his decisions in front of Congress

President B3: *Expand Presidential Rescission Powers, and Revive the Reorganization Act*

Also inspired by the No Labels Policy Playbook, both of these suggestions would slightly increase the president's ability to act, but in ways that would allow them to more appropriately fulfill their role as a check on the legislative branch (Congress). When it comes to congressional dysfunction, especially in regards to financial issues, the more power we can give to the president to break the gridlock and cut the bloat, the better.

Through the currently corrupt political processes of making laws, Congress often asks the president to sign spending bills that have numerous inefficient and excessive earmarks attached to the substantive core of the funding request. If the president were allowed expedited line-item rescission power, it would at least give a check to this political graft, providing the president an ability to quickly send back specific items on a bill for reconsideration by Congress. It is unconstitutional for the president to have straight line-item veto power, but rescission is basically the next best thing, forcing any specific items the president finds concerning to a congressional vote.

The Reorganization Act was passed in 1939 and allowed presidents the ability to eliminate and/or combine departments and agencies in the executive branch that were wasteful, inefficient, or redundant. There was congressional oversight to be a check on the process, but it allowed every President from FDR to Ronald Regan a more direct way to streamline and focus the government's function, reducing huge amounts of waste in the process. As a natural part of the bill's original structure, however, it expired in the 1980s. It would be very beneficial to bring this legislation back and restore the president's ability to immediately begin improving governmental efficiency as soon as they get into office.

So, what can you do? Any or all of the following...

1) Read the "No Labels Policy Playbook" at nolabels.org then speak to your friends and family on why helping a president to cut down on the waste and graft of Congress is a good idea.

2) Go to Change.org to start a petition (or citizen's initiative if your state allows) for granting the president expedited rescission powers and getting the *Reorganization Act* reintroduced to Congress. Their free online petition generator will not only allow you to easily draft the petition, but also get momentum by sending it out over social media prior to delivering it to your chosen governmental recipients.

Key Section Takeaways

We need to start thinking of ways to make the office of President function more efficiently, yet more in line with Constitutional parameters.

President B4: ***Tighten and Enumerate Anti-Corruption Standards for Presidents***

The need to make sure the president is singularly focused on working for the benefit of all Americans is crucial during their time in office—not themselves, their family, business partners or foreign powers. At one time in American history it seemed a generally accepted standard of ethics made this a very small concern, however, in recent years it has become more and more apparent that legislation is most likely needed to ensure the office of president can operate free of corrupting influences. Toward this end, it would be beneficial to pass Senator Elizabeth Warren's S 882 *Presidential Conflicts of Interest Act* into law.

The *Presidential Conflicts of Interest Act* (you can pull up a summary online) would require any president and vice president and their families to divest of conflicting assets through a blind trust, require presidential appointees to recuse themselves if any matter would substantially affect the president, and would prohibit the president and vice president from participating in federal contracts. In addition, this bill would require the president, vice president, and any major party nominee to be president or vice president to disclose their three most recent tax returns. All in all, this doesn't seem like too much to ask of someone trying to become the most powerful person in the world.

Additionally, there are even more detailed ideas for both preventing financial corruption of the executive branch and requiring more accountability, such as the proposals from the Brennan Center's *National Task Force on Rule of Law and Democracy*. Representative Katherine Clark is also sponsoring *HR 1481 The Presidential Accountability Act*. The most important thing at this juncture is to realize that there are currently many areas of potential abuse by the presidency, and to rein those in where possible and within reason.

So, what can you do? Any or all of the following...

1) Contact all your representatives to let them know that you want to make sure the office of president is uncorrupted. Demand they support S 882 *The Presidential Conflict of Interest Act, and/or HR 1481 The Presidential Accountability Act.* Use Azavea's technology (located at live.cicerodata.com), and go to this book's Sample Representative Letter to see and/or use an email template for sending to them.

2) Tell your friends and family that the *Presidential Conflict of Interest Act*, or something similar to it, is important to make sure the president works for us and not themselves. Or, just hand them this book, and have them sign up at **independ.me.**

Key Section Takeaways

It's probably time to clarify exactly what constitutes corruption by a President, so in the future no one can do something crazy... like operate their own business out of the White House and have their family make money from policy decisions.

Additional Actions for All Chapter Five Issues

In addition to the more specific sections suggestions listed in the proceeding chapter there are always three helpful general actions you can take at any time (below). It's also suggested to go to Appendix Three to check out additional bills in the current Congress that might be relevant to an issue.

1) Continue putting pressure on local, state, and federal representatives through directly emailing or calling to tell them stating you want one issue, or multiple ones, fixed. With Azavea's technology (located at https://live.cicerodata.com), you can quickly find the phone numbers and emails of everyone who represents you in all forms of government for free. You can even use this book's Sample Representative Letter (Appendix One) as an email template for sending to them.

2) If you are more ambitious to be a leader in reform, go to Change.org to start a petition (or a citizen's initiative if your state allows) for addressing the issue. A citizen's initiative is a petition that formally forces a legislative body to convene and vote on an issue (see Chap 9, Sec 8). Each state has its own rules and processes for starting a citizen's initiative, but regardless, you can get the ball rolling by easily starting a petition at change.org. Their system even helps you send your petition out to all your social media contacts.

3) Tell anyone and everyone about these issues and why they are important. This step is much more important than you might think, as the grassroots sharing of ideas is where all real change first happens. Or, simply give them this book or direct them to the other listed resources for more information. And sign up at independ.me for book updates, and subscribe to the "Independ Me" youtube channel.

Chapter Six

Freeing Our Politics from Money's Corruption, While Ensuring Free Speech

Money in politics is bad, right? In fact, according to a 2016 Rasmussen Reports poll, 80 percent of Americans believe money has too much influence on government. Whether in the left's calls for "Move to Amend," or the right's cries of "Drain the Swamp," reducing money's influence in politics seems to be about the only issue everyone in America agrees on. So why then does nothing ever get done? Because, the argument around what role money should have in politics is genuinely incredibly complex, and many politicians and special interests willfully use this complexity to keep things the way they are.

Hard money, soft money, lobbyists and the FEC, clean money, dark money, contribution and spending limits, PACs, 501(c)s, and *Citizens United*... a normal person wants to blow their brains out before wasting precious moments of their life on this crap. Just like with the tens of thousands of pages of needlessly convoluted IRS tax code, the only people who benefit from the insanely muddled campaign finance laws are the rich and powerful with the attorneys to navigate those very laws that are ostensibly designed to regulate them. Yet, its still important you kind of get what the gist of the real argument is.

If you'd like to read some specific examples of the political money tangle, check out Gregory Kreig's May, 2018, CNN article, "Legal? Yes. Ethical? Meh. Our Flimsy Lobbying and Campaign Finance Laws." Granted, the article leans toward primarily using Republican examples, but make no mistake that this is absolutely rampant in both parties. For even more indepth information regarding lobbying and campaign finance, check out podcast *Congressional Dish's* episodes 100 and 200.

Corrupt lawmakers on the right and left, and their wealthy, oligarchic benefactors, continue to reap the rewards, while your brainwashed neighbor parrots whatever his blue or red overlord tells him. Then you find it harder and harder to pay your electric bill, with the problems only getting worse as the decades of two-party abuse grinds on.

Since the *Citizens United* ruling in 2010, there has certainly been an explosion of funds into politics with OpenSecrets.org showing a tiny fraction of individuals (less than 1 percent of Americans) giving a whopping $1.18 billion to influence the 2014 elections, and that number continues to go up. According to Wikipedia, lobbying has been growing exponentially larger over the past 40 years, stating, "Since the 1970s, there has been explosive growth in the lobbying industry, particularly in Washington, DC. By 2011, one estimate of overall lobbying spending nationally was $30+ billion dollars. An estimate of lobbying expenses in the federal arena was $3.5 billion in 2010, while it had been only $1.4 billion in 1998." If you'd like to get a better understanding of how Washington lobbying has developed through intentionally poor regulation, the Center for Responsive Politics has some terrific resources on OpenSecrets.org succinctly showing its progression.

The goal of any political financial reform going forward should be to clearly, and simply, correct both campaign-finance issues and these systemic corruptions within the modern culture of Washington lobbying. If you've got even more time to take a deeper dive into all the concerns in our bizzaro system, you should probably start by reading professor Lawrence Lessig's seminal work on money in politics *Republic, Lost*. Luckily though, you don't have to become an expert in all this tediousness to have a bona fide opinion, you just need to grasp the legitimate core of the debate, which is the argument over ensuring free speech versus preventing political corruption.

This core debate, causing all the incessant noise from the right and left, rose to an apex in the infamous 2010 Supreme Court ruling of *Citizens United v FEC*. To quickly wrap your head around the infamous court case's meaning so that you can discuss these issues with anyone, just spend a few minutes watching a great *Hip Hughes* video by searching youtube.com for "Hip Hughes Citizens United Explained."

Suffice to say, money isn't always bad, and it realistically has to have some role in government. It can be used as both fuel for free speech (good) and political corruption (bad). For most in the blue jerseys, the *Citizen's United* ruling was an abomination of injustice at the highest order, blatantly allowing corporate corruption of our democracy. For most in the red jerseys though, this ruling was a rare victory for free speech and capitalism in an increasingly liberty-squelching country, a welcome example of First Amendment rights being upheld. The more you drop down the rabbit hole of partisan arguments though, the harder it honestly seems to say either side is entirely correct. Naturally, we need both less financial corruption in government, but also to ensure everyone's freedom of speech and right to petition their government is protected, the very difficult question is how to do it.

For example, consider that in a democracy everyone is supposed to have "speech," yet not everyone has money. That arguably means that someone with exponentially greater financial resources can drown out the voice of a less prosperous person, and how then can that possibly uphold the concept of the one-person, one-vote democracy that America is supposed to be? As Jen Briney points out in her episode 200 of *Congressional Dish*, once you factor in all the loopholes, a single rich individual can easily contribute nearly $1 million per election to the movement of their choice (with Republicans and Democrats allowed to receive substantially more than an independent). And rich individuals, families, and groups are absolutely doing it, with powerful effects on our government. Granted, there is a real concern for ensuring that anyone is allowed to reasonably spend their money in supporting the political ideas and the candidates they want, but the way current laws are set up is leading to the unavoidable side effect of people with more money having more "speech."

However, if we reflexively rush too far in the other direction in restricting certain people from spending their money in certain ways, we can quickly get into other very legitimate concerns. Who exactly gets to choose how much political "speech" each person gets through their money? Remember, everyone in the United States has a constitutional right to "petition" their government in the First Amendment. If people in power (government) at any time get to start choosing who can use their money for speech and petition, wouldn't that very process be subject to corrupted bias as well? It sounds like a great idea when the people you like are in power, but the very idea of democracy means they aren't always going to be in power, so do you really want whoever comes next to necessarily have the ability to determine who can spend what money supporting certain political causes and not others?

Even more difficult in American political finance laws might be in trying to sort out what exactly counts as "political free speech" or "petitioning" your government? Movies, T-shirts, dinners, commercials, paying for political rallies or parties? Or is maybe even giving your former Congressman a high-paying job for passing favorable legislation for your business? Shockingly, right now it is perfectly legal for you to give your former congressman a six-figure job if the laws he passed helped you, while you might have some trouble if you directly handed him that T-shirt (although you could still give it to someone at his party headquarters completely legally and they hand it over to him... moronic). Obviously, you can see how complex and circular the logic around this issue is, and start to get a general idea of how its getting exploited consistently, and with great effect, by the entrenched oligarchy of corrupted business people working in tandem with corrupted life-long Republican and Democrat professional politicians. So where and how do we draw the lines?

Despite what your red and blue t-shirt mouthpieces will try to convince you, this book will reiterate that both reducing money's influence on politics, and protecting free speech and the right for everyone to fairly petition their government, are equally important to ensuring the functioning of our democracy. And entirely doable. It just requires everyone to start understanding the issue a little more deeply and then honestly deciding what our standards of corruption actually are.

As John Adams said, "*Government is instituted for the common good: for the protection, safety, prosperity and happiness of the people, and not for profit, honor, or private interest of any one man, family, or class of men...*" Any lasting answer to the tangled questions earlier probably lie in first off agreeing on what the actual ideal is we are trying to achieve. This book would argue it is a one person, one vote democracy (popular sovereignty), not giving more political power to people just because they have more money. In a capitalistic society, richer people justifiably get to buy more material comfort than poorer people, but this does not mean they should be allowed to buy political power as well. Political power is the buffer against tyranny in a democracy, economic or otherwise. We should be fighting to label anything involving money that moves us away from equal political power for every American as corruption, even as we fight to help capitalism in business thrive... the two are not the same. Throughout history it can be seen that capitalism is far superior to any other economic model yet invented, but we must also remember that it can be manipulated. Government's function is not to replace capitalism, but it is to be it's umpire, and a game will never be fair if the umpires can get paid by one particular group of competitors. We need to start being more realistic about where regulations on capitalism should be drawn for maximum benefit for all. Wealthy people should be able to buy as many more big screen televisions than you as they see fit, but they shouldn't be able to buy laws. Again, capitalism is good for the economy, but not for a fair government.

The hard part comes on everyone understanding the issue enough to agree on what is best, without succumbing to political party buzzwords and bullshit. If you thought the proposed solutions for Gerrymandering were a sea of overtly complex politically-biased crap, just wait till you start trying to wade through all the proposal out their regarding money. The good news is that this issue continues to get more attention, and in the 116th Congress there are dozens, if not hundreds, of proposed bills trying to, or at least claiming to, address some issues of money's corrupting influence in our politics. With all the inherent complexity, and typical political duplicity involved, it gets very hard to whole-heartedly endorse a lot of so-called "solutions."

Case in point, the 116th Congressional Democrats *For the People* bill *HR 1*. This bill, if it were enacted into law, would certainly address many financial and election corruption concerns. However, it also has been claimed to have many Democrat-biased provisions woven into it's text, which has effectively kept any Republicans from supporting it. Currently at around 700 pages long, it is no wonder that its chances of passing are slim, and that the potential for party-biased shenanigans are rife within it. 700 pages! If anyone were serious about actually passing financial, ethics, or election reforms, it seems like they would be trying to make it as simple and straightforward as possible, in order to have it stand at least some chance of becoming law. Unfortunately, a 700 page beast of legal mumbo-jumbo seems to have served more of a purpose of the Democrats being able to take up a false banner of moral superiority, without actually having to do anything to change the precious system they are part of. This is not to say there are not some Democrats, and even Republicans, genuinely fighting for financial, ethical, and electoral reforms, but that failure on both sides for *HR 1* is a prime example of the systemic corruption and dysfunction that now pervades our government.

This book would argue that the key is to now stop making things more tangled on this issue, but to enact sharp, straight ethical reforms cutting through all the absurdly complex legal and philosophical arguments. We will present the more reputable options for financial reform we have found, but toward the issue of simplicity, are actually endorsing a couple. Please research the others listed on your own, and determine if they fit with your own ideals and understanding enough to support.

The goal of any reforms should never be to have one side gain advantage over another, whether they were a red shirt, a blue shirt, or a purple shirt. The goal should be a one person, one vote popular sovereignty in this country, with no amount of money ever distorting that democratic distribution of power, and everyone able to freely exercise their speech.

Money A1: *Campaign Finance Reform*

Money currently has a massive influence on who gets elected in this country, with the richest being able to have the most influence. To protect one person, one vote democracy, we need to fix this so all individuals have closer to equal weight. There are so many competing groups, movements, and ideas focused on campaign finance at this time that it would probably be counterproductive to list them all, only exacerbating the complexity rather than getting us closer to a solution. Because of both the power and simplicity of their goal, this book only currently supports two movements for campaign finance reform, *American Promise* and *Represent.Us*. Additional movements and 116th bills are listed at the end of the section for your consideration though.

AmericanPromise.net is a nonpartisan group of individuals supporting passage of a Twenty-eighth Amendment to the United States Constitution that will provide a straightforward and lasting standard for campaign finance issues. According to the group's website:

"*Our Goal*

American Promise is leading the charge to win the 28th Amendment so We the People—not big money, not corporations, not unions, not special interests—govern the United States of America.

The Amendment process is well on its way to help set reasonable spending limits in our political elections, so that all Americans—regardless of net worth—can take responsibility for our lives, govern ourselves, and honor our national destiny.

Our Mission

American Promise exists to empower, inspire, and organize Americans to win the 28th Amendment to the Constitution. This lasting reform will re-balance our politics and government by putting the rights of individual citizens before the privileges of concentrated money, corporations, unions, political parties, and superPACs.

Our Vision

A healthy, just, and lasting American republic, in which Constitutional rights for human beings are secure, and all citizens are equal, with the right and the responsibility to govern effectively together."

American Promise is already gaining steam across the nation, and unlike many other reform movements, they are taking great strides to use nonpartisan logic and reason to solidify their proposed changes. Their goal is not to form a new party, or to benefit one of the existing parties over another; they simply intend the one-item objective of actually getting a Twenty-eighth Amendment passed.

They are so committed to creating a viable solution that works for all Americans, they are even still taking suggestions from anyone and everyone through their online poll on the actual language and issues addressed in the amendment as long as they subscribe to: "1) secure fair, free elections; 2) protect the rights of all Americans to equal participation and representation; and 3) return to original liberties for people rather than new privileges for the largest corporations, unions, and special interests."

Where and how exactly these goals are achieved can still be influenced by you, once you sign up and get involved. *American Promise* intends to achieve their goal by by-passing Congress and calling a state-based Article V convention (read about the process in Chap 9, Sec 5). And once a Twenty-eighth Amendment is passed, it will hopefully permanently reinforce the one person, one vote ideal our democracy was created on, forever stopping right-versus-left wrangling over who gets to be financially corrupted the most.

Represent.Us is an extremely vibrant organization rapidly gaining steam across the country. They have a brilliant idea to take care of corruption from the exact opposite end of the political spectrum, through getting their *American Anti-Corruption Act* passed on the local and state levels everywhere, thereby circumventing the need for a corrupt federal government to even be involved. You should definitely go to their website to watch their videos like "Unbreaking America" and "How to Fix America's Broken Political System" amongst others. Part of their brilliance of their idea is having the support system in place to help you, yes you, tailor the *American Anti-Corruption Act* to get passed in your own area. What's great, is that both *American Promise* and the *American Anti-Corruption Act* could be worked on at the same time, as well as contacting your representatives to tell them to support some of the proposed legislation within the 116th Congress.

Currently, the amendments proposed within the Congress include Senator Tom Udall's *S 51 Democracy for All*, Senator Jon Tester's *S 736*, Rep Adam Schiff's *HJ Res 57*, Rep John Yarmuth's *HJ Res 33*, Rep Kurt Schrader's *HJ Res 21*, and Rep Ted Deutch's *HJ Res 2*.

Additionally, there are other nationwide groups attempting to call Article V conventions to bypass Congress with a constitutional amendment, including *Move to Amend*, *Wolf-Pac*, *Fix It America*, and *Take Back Our Republic*. Some have slightly different ideas on how to handle the corrupt-money versus free speech issue, so you should certainly decide for yourself which you will support. A multi-prong approach will ensure that results happen either on the Constitutional end, the Congress, or through local and state governments.

And last, an often overlooked area of needed reform is in updating and removing the problems that exists in the *Federal Elections Commission*. This is the regulatory body of government that is in charge of overseeing and enforcing elections and campaign finance law. Being small, ineffective and largely made up of Republican and Democratic insiders, it is at best incompetent for its purpose, and possibly corrupt. Luckily, bipartisan reform group *Issue One* has gotten two bills sponsored called *HR 1272 Restoring Integrity to America's Elections, and HR 679 Political Accountability and Transparency Act*. Supporting these bills' passages into law is a straightforward way to make real progress in improving our overall financial corruption problem.

So what should you do? Any or all of the following...

1) Go to AmericanPromise.net right now and sign up. Take their online poll to give your immediate input as to what is most important to you regarding how the Twenty-eighth Amendment is structured, then see what else you can do to lend support. Spread the word to your friends and family about American Promise, and direct them to the website.

2) Go to Represent.Us right now and sign up. Watch their videos, learn about their *American Anti-Corruption Act*, and consider getting involved.

3) Contact your representatives and tell them you want them to support the passage of *HR 1272 Restoring Integrity to America's Elections* and *HR 679 Political Accountability and Transparency Act*

4) Go to the Center for Responsive Politics' OpenSecrets.org website, and followthemoney.org, to sign up for their newsletters to stay informed about Washington corruption.

5) Consider contacting your governmental representatives to tell them to support any or all of the following Constitutional amendments proposed in the 116th Congress: *S51 Democracy for All Udall, s 736 Tester, HJ Res 57 Schiff, HJ Res 33 Yarmuth, HJ Res 21 Schrader, HJ Res 2 Deutch.*

6) Look at, and consider supporting, some of the other groups looking to call an Article V convention to cure the issue of money corrupting politics, including... MovetoAmend.org, wolf-pac.org, fixitamerica.org, takeback.org

7) Sign up at IssueOne.org to see what you can do to help get corrupt money out of politics.

Key Section Takeaways

Our polarization will never be completely fixed until we stop the corruption of the two-party system. We can do this through *American Promise* and the *American Anti-Corruption Act*

Money B1: *Reforming Lobbying*

So, chances are, the person you last voted for to protect your interests in the US government is right now listening to a guy who works for a corporation or special interest. That lobbyist is hinting (pseudo-legally) at how wealthy the congressman or woman will become if they just pass laws favorable to their particular client, rather than you. That's the bulk of the way government now works.

Around $3 billion a year is typically now spent on lobbying a year with a 2004 University of Kansas study showed that a typical corporate dollar spent on lobbying for favorable tax treatment actually showed an amazing 22,000 percent return for the businesses hiring those lobbyists! That's a vast amount of cash flowing from businesses to governmental employees, and those businesses receiving an amazing return, for anyone to actually try claiming that the government isn't corrupted by money. So, even once *American Promise* gets a concise and powerful Twenty-eighth Amendment to permanently fix campaign finance, the tricky issue of lobbying will most likely still need additional restraints.

Although campaign finance and lobbying concerns certainly overlap, unethical issues within the world of lobbying infect far more than just campaigning, including the actual laws that are passed and how governmental agencies enforce laws and regulations. Lobbying in Washington, DC is the ill-gotten food that sustains the corrupt beast.

If you've got time for a fascinating overview of how DC lobbying works from an insider who used to do it, listen to episode one hundred of amazing Jen Briney's *Congressional Dish* podcast interviewing convicted felon Jack Abramoff. Or, read the insightful and succinct *Vox* article by former lobbyist Jimmy Williams on specific examples of how bribery is pretty much legal in Washington today. You can also read Lee

Drutman's article in *The Atlantic* about how lobbying influence has dramatically increased since the 1970s.

Suffice to say, in America, people with money currently get laws passed for them even if those laws aren't the will of the majority. American politicians are getting rich and powerful off of doing the bidding of corporations and wealthy special interest groups, often to the determent of the very people they have sworn to represent. And, most shocking of all, in our modern America it is not that outright bribery no longer exists, but it has mostly been made legal by the very two parties that currently benefits from it.

The areas of most concern include:

1) *The laws against bribing and financially corrupting policymakers are laughably convoluted and under-enforced.* We must reform the laws so that lobbyists simply cannot make direct political donations to candidates or parties, give gifts, or provide myriad other financial incentives like investment tips or favorable corporate treatment.

2) *Washington is a massive revolving door of employment between government and business.* It must be permanently shut. Currently, wealthy businesses are legally allowed to promise lucrative careers and investments to "friendly" members of Congress and government agencies able to influence legislation to benefit their companies or industries. We must institute firm bans on politicians and government officials leaving their offices or agencies for high-paying jobs in industries their governmental positions impacted or were associated with.

3) *There is no independent, non-partisan and non-political, agency to strictly oversee and enforce ethics in government that actually functions well.* Most of this regulation falls within the jurisdiction of the FEC (*Federal Election Commission*), but this organization is largely driven by

partisan political goals and hampered by inadequate structure. We need an effective, politically independent agency once and for all to enforce the ethical requirements of government.

4) *And speaking of governmental agencies, many of those tasked with overseeing the regulation of industries are as awash in corporate influence as the lawmakers themselves.* Often, the companies supposedly being regulated are the very same ones who have the most input on what their industry's regulations are. Some of their input is necessary and reasonable, but there must be reforms to make sure the non-wealthy public's interest is also "lobbied" for, not just the small groups of people positioning to get rich from the outcome.

Luckily, Democratic Senator Elizabeth Warren has already created an extensive *s 3357 Anti-Corruption and Integrity Act* in the 115th Congress that addresses most of the above concerns. Right-versus-left dogma will try to take a stance on these suggestions by saying it is capitalism versus socialism, but that is simply not the case, or at least not need to be. For a capitalist society to retain legitimacy so it can function at its ideal level, it must have some real anti-corruption regulation. As is a theme throughout this book, Republicans nor Democrats are correct all the time, but occasionally individuals from either side have ideas that might be appropriate for the times. Currently, in issues of financial corruption, it seems some Democrats have it more correct.

Warren's anti-corruption bill is the first in modern history to attempt to deal with almost all aspects of the lobbying issue. It may be a long shot to get passed in its current, utterly game-changing form, but it still serves as an excellent "North Star" for what any other reforms should attempt, even if it initially fails. A copy of her mastery summary of the bill's proposals is available on her website, and it will hopefully be re-introduced in the 116th. It is strongly encouraged you support it, or a bill much like it, passing into law.

So what should you do? Any and all of the following...

1) Put pressure on local, state, and federal representatives through directly emailing or calling to demand an end to Washington lobbying corruption. Thanks to Azavea's technology (located at https://live.cicerodata.com), you can insist they support the reforms listed in Senator Warren's *s 3357 Anti-Corruption and Integrity Act* from the 115th Congress.

2) Listen to podcasts such as Jen Briney's *Congressional Dish* episode 100 and 200, and *Decode DC*, in order *to* better understand how Washington works to benefit itself rather than you. In fact, if you've got the time, even read Lawrence Lessig's book *Republic, Lost*.

3) And also take a few minutes to watch Abby Martin's 2014 video on youtube discussing President Dwight Eisenhower's speech warning against the rise of the military-industrial complex. It is better to not let yourself slip too far down any conspiracy rabbit holes with this stuff, but just consider how common-sense ethical and corruption reform in government could improve things.

Key Section Takeaways

Lobbying is the corrupt practice of people with more money than you getting preferential treatment from government, and it is making your life suck.

Additional Actions for All Chapter Six Issues

In addition to the more specific sections suggestions listed in the proceeding chapter there are always three helpful general actions you can take at any time (below). It's also suggested to go to Appendix Three to check out additional bills in the current Congress that might be relevant to an issue.

1) Continue putting pressure on local, state, and federal representatives through directly emailing or calling to tell them stating you want one issue, or multiple ones, fixed. With Azavea's technology (located at https://live.cicerodata.com), you can quickly find the phone numbers and emails of everyone who represents you in all forms of government for free. You can even use this book's Sample Representative Letter (Appendix One) as an email template for sending to them.

2) If you are more ambitious to be a leader in reform, go to Change.org to start a petition (or a citizen's initiative if your state allows) for addressing the issue. A citizen's initiative is a petition that formally forces a legislative body to convene and vote on an issue (see Chap 9, Sec 8). Each state has its own rules and processes for starting a citizen's initiative, but regardless, you can get the ball rolling by easily starting a petition at change.org. Their system even helps you send your petition out to all your social media contacts.

3) Tell anyone and everyone about these issues and why they are important. This step is much more important than you might think, as the grassroots sharing of ideas is where all real change first happens. Or, simply give them this book or direct them to the other listed resources for more information. And sign up at independ.me for book updates, and subscribe to the "Independ Me" youtube channel.

Chapter Seven

Freeing the Supreme Court and State Governments from Polarization and Corruption

When most people think of America's government, they tend to think of the president and then Congress. It's true that these two areas comprise most of America's national decision-making as well as receive the most news coverage, but there are a couple of other very important parts of American government. The Constitution purposely designed America's entire government to function best when the judicial branch (Supreme Court) and every individual state's government play a role. The executive (president) and legislative (Congress) branches are certainly designed to have the most national powers, but the courts and states are ideally supposed to serve as checks and balances to those first two.

Objectively, there is legitimate debate over what the Supreme Court and states' roles should be, but it is important to understand that any and all laws and procedures are the result of prior debates between mortal humans just like us. You can join these debates at any time, if you wish to change things to work better or be fairer. For American government to function at its best, it is critical that citizens understand the roles of the Supreme Court and the states, and fight to keep their rights and abilities. This can best be done by removing artificial two-party influence over them, while enhancing everyone's awareness of their inherent Constitutional powers and roles. For those of us who wish to keep corruption and partisanship to a minimum, the states and the courts offer the most powerful way to balance any wayward federal government.

The Supreme Court

Maybe because of the complexity of distilling its actions down to easily conveyed sounds bites on the news, the Supreme Court often does not appear as important for average Americans as Congress or the presidency? Maybe it also has something to do with the fact that it is entirely made up of people who look like your grandparents wearing bath robes? Regardless, it's still important to know that the Supreme Court (with Federal and appellate courts) comprises the crucial third branch of federal American government, the judicial.

Three is a powerful number. Unlike two, which can collude and work together for nefarious ends, three is a natural antiseptic against corruption, as there is always a much greater chance that at least one will not go along with the other two. Our founding fathers did not create three branches of government by accident—each is a crucial leg of support for our democratic-republic. The nine members of the Supreme Court are essentially the highest and last authority on interpreting whether those laws and actions spawned from the other two branches of American government are in line with the meaning and/or purpose of the Constitution.

As Alexander Hamilton noted in *Federalist 78*, the Supreme Court is not designed to have the power of the sword or the purse, but they do have the ability to call for restraint through their judgment, whenever either of those two is used in opposition to our agreed upon highest legal document, the Constitution. Hamilton explained, "*[A] limited Constitution... can be preserved in practice no other way than through the medium of courts of justice, whose duty it must be to declare all acts contrary to the manifest tenor of the Constitution void. Without this, all the reservations of particular rights or privileges would amount to nothing...*"

An important point that is often overlooked in modern

discussions is that the courts were assumed to have an inherent bias toward limiting federal government overreach and keeping it in check. Being the interpreter and final judge of the actions of those other two more political, elected branches, the judicial was created from the beginning to be as nonpolitical as possible, rather than motivated by faction or personal power. That said, the actual specific functions of the Supreme Court, as in what decisions it has jurisdiction to make and what its motivations and goals in making those decisions should be, have been the source of raging political debate and attempted manipulation since the founding of the country to this very day.

If interested, you can go all the way back to the 1803 Supreme Court ruling of Marbury v Madison to see that somebody has pretty much thought the court was doing things wrong since its inception. Many people with a conservative outlook believe Supreme Court review of laws should be more limited, always erring on the side of strict, minimalist interpretation of specific words from the Constitution and its framers' "original intent." Many of a more liberal slant, however, see the Supreme Court as a proactive philosophical agent of change, and encourage that the Supreme Court should be working in a more "activist" way to override the errors of society (and the other two branches of government) wherever they find them through a "living," and therefore a more subjective and always evolving, Constitution.

Delving with intelligent consideration into the pros and cons of these extremes is beyond the scope of our discussion, so we'd suggest you start with an excellent and succinct 2004 summary from the American Bar Association by Barbara Perry called *Original Intent or Evolving Constitution*, then try to listen and read a variety of positions on the subject to create your own conclusion, including *Federalist 78*. In the meantime, the official position of this book on where we should draw the line between these two classical "original intent" or "living Constitution" roles for the Supreme Court, is... at this point inconclusive. We can at least ensure the Supreme Court is as nonpolitical, independent, and free of corruption as possible while the debate continues about the deeper questions.

The suggested reforms in this section are not to give the Supreme Court more or less power, or a more conservative or liberal mandate, but to simply protect it from any political agenda over the long term, enhance its autonomy, and just like with all other sections of American government, combat its potential for corruption. Whatever end goals (more conservative, more progressive, etc..) you end up deciding are best for the Supreme Court to employ, they will only be able to achieve these if they are free and independent from the political influences of two-party oligarchs, and their potential for corruption. This book's position for the Supreme Court, as with the other two branches of government, is that transparency, diversification of power, and frequently transferring who holds it as much as possible, is pretty much always a good thing.

Here are the best ideas on how we can do that.

Courts A1: *Impose Term Limits on The Supreme Court*

It's strange to think that we actually have any lifetime appointments in American government, which is still the way the Supreme Court operates for its nine justices. The whole idea of America was to be done with lifetime monarchs and the inevitable corruption, dysfunction, and inequity that comes with such systems. Yet, once confirmed, all nine of the Supreme Court justices have always enjoyed lifetime appointments.

This was primarily done to ensure that one branch of government would be somewhat immune from the vagaries and short-term influences of day-to-day political power plays. The reasoning was that if the justices did not need to solicit votes to get and retain their positions, and they could not be removed based on changing political tides within the other two branches, we'd have a much higher chance of having a judicial branch solely focused on preserving the letter and spirit of the Constitution. The reasoning is sound, and despite the debates over the wisdom of the court's specific conclusions, it is obviously the least political and most ethical of all American branches of government. That said, it could still be improved.

Imposing term limits, as long as they are still of a substantially longer term than any other position in the other two branches, would ensure the same inoculation to political whims of the day necessary, and lessen the court's own chances of internal corruption. Term limits would help ensure new, robust thinking was continually circulating through its halls through regular new appointments. It's not really a radical idea, it just sort of makes common sense, and limiting any one individual to something like eighteen years seems like plenty of time to serve.

It is relevant to note that in Colonial times average life expectancy was not as long, so arguably a lifetime appointment then was expected to be closer to twenty years of service, rather than the forty- to fifty-year terms modern justices are now serving with greater and greater frequency. Not only is it more likely for people to abuse power or become lazy in its dutiful execution, if it is given to them with no chance of ever being taken away, there are also real issues of a single individual, whether from age or disinterest, being able to stay in tandem with society enough to provide wise council for its current concerns. A single, nonrenewable eighteen-year term for each Supreme Court justice would be ideal, still providing a long enough stretch of service to easily be outside the whims of any political changes in the other two branches, yet short enough to ensure that the court was always filled with robust, engaged individuals.

An eighteen-year term limit would not only ensure a healthy turnover of new justices and new perspective on the court, it would also help lessen the political partisanship that has attempted to infect it through modern times. From the recent 2018 circus of Judge Brett Kavanaugh's confirmation, back to Justice Clarence Thomas, it seems both the right and left are making the process of selecting the court more and more dysfunctional and political, each attempting to squeeze more extreme, and therefore less impartial, justices in whenever they can.

It is still ideal that the president, as the people's elected leader, gets to nominate who will sit on the court whenever there is a vacancy, but with all subject to an eighteen-year term it would mean those vacancies would come with much more regularity across multiple presidencies. Essentially, each seat could be rotated to have one becoming vacant every two years, ensuring every president would get to slightly alter the court according to his mandate. Barring illness, death, or unforeseen retirement, however, no president would be allowed to drastically "pack" the court with a majority of justices conspiring to his most extreme positions.

Once again, it would be best for us to place our trust in the diversification and rotation of power, especially in our branch of government that serves as such a vital check to the other two, and often influences social norms and legal precedent for generations to come. There's really no reasonable argument for not doing it.

So, what can you do? Any and all of the following...

1) Go to FixTheCourt.com and sign up to help them force reforms

2) Contact all your representatives to let them know that you want to make the court less political through imposing eighteen-year term limits on justices. Use Azavea's technology (located at https://live.cicerodata.com) and this book's Sample Representative Letter.

4) Tell your friends and family how installing eighteen-year term limits on the Supreme Court would help it be less political and function better. Or, just hand them this book, and have them register at **independ.me**.

Key Section Takeaways

It would help everything regarding our legislative branch of government to install term limits on its office holders.

Courts A2: *Clarify Court's Mandate*

The proper role of the Supreme Court has been debated since the country's inception. Should the court always be reinterpreting the often sparse language of the Constitution to the concerns of today in a "living," and therefore potentially changing Constitutional concept, as most progressives argue for? It might sound good at first, however, the degree to which this concept is applied can possibly turn a lifesaving medicine into a deadly poison. If the only set of rules we can reference for how things are supposed to work can continually change, do we really have any agreed upon rules at all, or is just always up to whoever happens to hold the power?

The opposite position, probably leading to an ineffectual third branch of federal government in the extreme, is to employ a strict "constructionist" view of the Constitution, and thereby an incredibly restrained idea of the Supreme Court's ability to interfere with the other branches of government. The conservatives who mostly champion this view believe the court should be very limited in what laws it can review, and its decisions solely based on the letter of the Constitution, and the best guess of its exact meaning when agreed upon over 250 years ago. Obviously though, this can lead to challenges that might have no good resolution as society and technology evolve through the centuries and leave the Supreme Court an impotent third wheel for keeping up with modern culture. Additionally, although this book often takes the position of choosing to limit governmental power instead of expanding it, the Supreme Court's judicial review does inherently offer an opportunity to "do good" in ways that the more political and bureaucratic branches can't, or won't.

This book doesn't know the exact answer, but would suggest it's maybe time for us to collectively create one. It is notable that the Article III of the Constitution is the shortest of the three explaining how each branch is supposed to function, and arguably gives no clear guidance on what lens the justices should be using to perform their judicial review functions. Should they be proactively attempting to uphold justice? Equality? Fairness? The exact and original meaning of the Constitution and nothing else? Only those rights listed in the Constitution, or fighting to make the country a better place? And then, of course, "better" according to who? Maybe it is time for a constitutional amendment clarifying exactly what the Supreme Court's role and guiding principle should be.

Rather than suggesting you fight for some defined mandate right now, we'd just suggest you learn a bit more about the arguments (like the Barbara Perry article mentioned earlier) and why the need for clarification is there. Once you feel like you understand the basics, you can explain it to your friends and family, and maybe over time, a conclusive and more defined mandate for the courts can rise up from us all. In the meantime, we'd humbly suggest it might have something to do with protecting every citizen's popular sovereignty and free will.

Key Section Takeaway

It's probably time to actually clarify, and put in writing, exactly what the goals of the Supreme Court should be

The States

The federal government was only ever given power by the individual states all agreeing to it through the Constitution. What constitutes the jurisdiction of the federal government, versus each state's government, is addressed in the Constitution's Supremacy Clause and the Tenth Amendment, yet has been debated since the dawn of the country by those very people creating it.

The Supremacy Clause states: "*This Constitution, and the Laws of the United States which shall be made in Pursuance thereof; and all Treaties made, or which shall be made, under the Authority of the United States, shall be the supreme Law of the Land; and the Judges in every State shall be bound thereby, any Thing in the Constitution or Laws of any State to the Contrary notwithstanding.*"

While the Tenth Amendment adds: "*The powers not delegated to the United States by the Constitution, nor prohibited by it to the States, are reserved to the States respectively, or to the people.*"

To anyone not looking to manipulate the system to their own advantage, the culmination of these two constitutional explanations, on where the demarcation line between federal and state powers lies, clearly means that the federal government reigns supreme over all states' governments, but only in those powers expressly written in the Constitution. However, because of the inherent vagueness of these constitutional instructions to the myriad of possible real-life scenarios arising within a country of fifty separate states, and hundreds of millions of separate individuals, the argument on the ideal way for our federal and state governments to work together still gets justifiably complex. To start getting your head around the potential modern arguments, think about some of these things:

• Currently, around ten states (led by Colorado) have made marijuana legal within its borders, yet it is still illegal anywhere within America according to the federal government. So, are people using weed in these states criminals or not? Keep in mind this precedent could easily be applied to numerous other issues like abortion, gun rights, or gay marriage.

• At one point a president (Andrew Jackson) almost invaded a state (South Carolina) with the US Army because the state disrespected his decision (in what is historically referred to as the Nullification Crisis). Should it be legal for presidents to use the military to take over a state if they want?

• Everyone knows about the Civil War, but there have actually been dozens of prominent movements for different states to remove themselves from America leading right up until today. In our democracy, if a majority of a state's people vote to no longer be part of the United States, should they be allowed to leave, or is this treason?

• The European Union is made up of separate countries like Germany, France, and Spain, who retain their own autonomous governments and militaries but join together in a set of rules governing them all. Some of the founding fathers wanted the United States to function more like this, with each state almost its own independent "nation." Would we be better or worse off if this were the case?

The arguments around where federal and state governmental powers begin and end in America, on every issue from taxation and business regulation to criminal law, is fascinating and possibly infinitely complex. We'd suggest it is a very beneficial area to think about going forward, as it could offer some unique and overlooked solutions to a myriad of modern issues with our overall government function.

To get a deeper understanding of this core debate of federal versus state's rights you should learn about the Kentucky and Virginia Resolutions of 1798. In them, Thomas Jefferson and James Madison argued that the states should, and already do, have the ability to nullify any unconstitutional laws made by the federal government. In today's climate of federal dysfunction and corruption, this concept serves as a much-needed potential solution.

Taken to an extreme, however, the "principles of '98" argument could be very problematic. Through the history of the US, the term "states' rights" has taken on a repugnant stain, often being invoked to keep inhumane and racist policies such as in the 1960s civil rights clashes and leading up to the Civil War. However, the same principles are now being used to fight for more traditionally progressive platforms, like legalization or weed, and combating climate change. So which is it, do the states each have any sovereign power, or is the federal government sovereign in all matters over the states? And independent of being on the red team or the blue team, where would the best line be to protect democracy for all, and optimize the function of checks and balances in our country's overall government?

We'd argue the goal should not be to protect absolute federal sovereignty, or absolute state sovereignty, but realize it is always the correct combination of the two, each limiting the other's powers, which can serve as the proper checks and balances necessary to ensure the popular sovereignty of every American individual's inherent rights and freedoms over any form of government. Just to warn you though, even the term "popular sovereignty" was briefly used to try to protect keeping slavery alive in some US territories, but we should not let racists hijack a crucial concept for protecting all of our liberties.

Protecting the popular sovereignty of the people (in simplistic terms, everyone's free will) should be the goal over fighting for either federal or state dominance. And we should strive for any and all reforms to improve balance between the two governments, which in this day of increasingly powerful federal government, probably means fighting for a little more state's rights.

As Alexander Hamilton explained in *Federalist 28*, "*In a confederacy the people, without exaggeration, may be said to be entirely the masters of their own fate. Power being almost always the rival of power; the General Government will at all times stand ready to check the usurpations of the state governments; and these will have the same disposition toward the General Government. The people, by throwing themselves into either scale, will infallibly make it preponderate. If their rights are invaded by either, they can make use of the other, as the instrument of redress.*"

So how do we help ensure popular sovereignty for all Americans? By doing two things: A) fighting for increasing individual states' modern powers to be slightly more in line with original Constitutional ideals and B) fighting to end the national two-party-system's control of your individual state, so more uncorrupted people can lead in it.

States A1: *Understand and Discuss the Issues*

As mentioned above, states' rights versus federal power is a complex issue going all the way back to the original debates over how the country should be designed. Honestly, a lot of the issues were never really adequately resolved, and they now affect everything from the laws and taxes you are subject to, to how people are elected, to national security and your individual rights as an American citizen. If there is anything you can do as a true independent to best help this issue, it's probably to understand it on a bit deeper level and form your own opinions as to where you stand.

A robust group fighting for states' rights is the Los Angeles-based *Tenth Amendment Center* (tenthamendmentcenter.com). They have a wealth of articles and resources framed from a perspective of how things could be improved by demanding our government to adhere to the Tenth Amendment protecting states' rights. Additionally, Libertarian groups and thinkers are typically great arguers for enhancing states' rights (see books below), if you want to give them a listen or read. You may not end up agreeing with all of their positions, but it might help you see things in new ways. And as mentioned earlier, the historic *Kentucky and Virginia Resolutions of 1798* really set the whole precedent on this debate, if you don't mind taking a deeper dive into Constitutional history.

You should be careful, however, in just blindly jumping on any bandwagon that uses the phrase "states' rights." There are still many bigoted and extremist groups in the country that hide behind the idea of "states' rights" as they did leading up to the Civil War, and a lot of people who get themselves into substantial trouble with the IRS over it in trying to avoid all taxes. It's important that you learn about, and discuss, this issue with reason and moderation. There are also movements within this issue which this book does not support, like repealing the Seventeenth Amendment to make senators appointed by state governments rather than elected by the people. Again, it is this book's humble opinion that your goal should maybe not be to fight for either absolute federal or state dominance in all areas, but fight for the goal of enhancing states' rights to serve primarily as another avenue for enhancing all people's individual freedom, from each other, and any form of government.

So what can you do? Any or all of the following...

1) Go to the Tenth Amendment Center to learn more about this issue and maybe sign up with them.

2) Read and learn about this issue through the web and books like:

> *The Politically Incorrect Guide to American History* by Tom Woods
>
> *Reclaiming the American Revolution* by William Watkins
>
> *The Politically Incorrect Guide to the Constitution* by Kevin Gutzman

Then make up your own mind on how things should be.

3) Once you've learned and thought about the issue, bring it up to your friends and family so they understand its importance, or just hand them this book. Also, sign up at independ.me to stay up to date with future versions of the book.

Key Section Takeaways

The states offer a under-utilized, but extremely powerful, way to enhance check and balances to federal government over-reach. Its time to think about using them.

States A2: *Ask Your Representatives to Think About States' Rights in a Modern Way*

Although restoring a more appropriate balance between state and federal government power tends to be something more people on the political right publicly support, it is an important nonpartisan concept that should concern everyone.

A powerful group attempting to make elected representatives aware of this issue is the *American Legislative Exchange Council* (ALEC). Unfortunately, although successful at empowering state's legislatures to fight for their autonomy, this group is arguably often doing it to primarily benefit the corporate oligarchy structure this book is trying to fight. According to their website: "The American Legislative Exchange Council is America's largest nonpartisan voluntary membership organization of state legislators dedicated to the principles of limited government, free markets and federalism." You can visit a site called alecexposed.org to show the argument against them.

Whether or not they are using their skills for good or evil, in organizing and focusing state legislatures to be more powerful, is currently beyond the scope of this version of the book. Rather, they are brought up as an example of what could possibly be done, if all groups and individuals started to realize the power of states' rights. Imagine, for instance, if groups with more altruist purpose than just corporate greed used the same tactics as ALEC to robustly participate in state legislative procedure? We might actually start to get to the kind of democratic-republic of checks and balances our founding fathers thought they were originally designing.

You can check out information for and against ALEC to determine if they are good or evil on your own, but regardless you can still use their handy *Resolution of State Sovereignty* (available on their website) template to provide your representatives with a starting point for fighting for state's rights in issues you care about.

So what should you do? Any or all of the following...

1) Check out both alec.org and alecexposed.org, and think about how state legislatures can be a powerful force in government for good and bad, then maybe contact your representatives to find out where they stand on states' rights and if concept is being used to the best benefit.

Key Section Takeaways

You can start thinking about the benefits of state's rights, how to use them properly, and then spread the ideas to other people, including your own political representatives

States B1: *Research Electoral and Governance Issues in Your Own State*

With fifty different states, each with its own myriad laws and electoral processes, it is far beyond the scope of this book to suggest specific reforms for all of them. Instead, we would encourage you to gain a deeper understanding of the relevant issues in your own state. You can also fight for some general principles that will certainly help lessen the two-party's corrupt grip wherever you are.

Like almost everything in modern American politics, state electoral issues tend to be promoted on prefabricated red-versus-blue talking points. If you listen to a Republican, they will say "securing" the integrity of elections is of utmost importance, while if you listen to a Democrat, they will say that ensuring no Americans are "suppressed" when they go to vote is the major concern. Once again, the reality is that both positions are incomplete, as we need both voting security and an ability to ensure all American citizens can participate. The oversimplified talking points only serve to help both sides of the two parties stay in power over the long term. The reality is that we don't need private groups (Republicans or Democrats) in charge of our elections at all, and things would drastically change for the better if the two-party system was not allowed to continue pulling the strings to our elections.

Law professor Gilda Daniels has written about how America has oddly allowed the control of our elections fall completely within the power of two private institutions (Republicans and Democrats) in *Outsourcing Democracy*, and so it is inevitable that they will be the ones getting elected. From the governmental officials in charge of regulating elections, down to the poll workers checking your ID and handing you a ballot, almost all of these people are solely appointed by the political party they are sworn to serve. Check out Rick Hasen's *Talking Points Memo* article regarding this issue, or his book *The Voting Wars*, for even more detailed information on how our modern election process has been completely hijacked by the two parties. If something isn't done to quickly address removing elections from the hands of the two-party oligarchs to nonpartisan overseers, it is extremely likely we will have increasing election crises in the future, and undermine the legitimacy of our democracy even further.

So what can you do? Any or all of the following...

1) Learn as much as you can about how the two-party system controls elections in your specific state. You can start by reading Gilda Daniels' article "Outsourcing Democracy" as well as Rick Hasen's book *The Voting Wars*, then research what dysfunctions might currently be going on in your area.

2) You can go to the websites of organization's like FairVote.org, Ballotpedia.org, and BrennanCenter.org to find interactive maps giving a lot of information about your legislation and processes in your particular state.

2) Consider joining Let America Vote. Granted, the organization is left-leaning, ostensibly motivated by the fact that larger minority turnout leads to greater probabilities of Democrats getting elected, but there is also a potential nonpartisan benefit if the group serves to keep elections more open and transparent at the local level.

Key Section Takeaways

Given that most state's control their own election processes, you can have a tremendous impact to ending two-party corruption by fighting to end it in your own area.

States B2: *Demand Your State's Election Officials Renounce Any Party Affiliation*

Over two-thirds of American states still allow the primary governmental official in charge of overseeing elections to be appointed by the political party that last won. This is exactly as problematic as it sounds, with a party-loyal secretary of state or lieutenant governor doubtful in their impartiality toward determining the results of any future election their party competes in. You wouldn't let the referee of a football game be a member of either team would you, so why continue to allow this?

In the infamously narrow Presidential election of 2000, Florida Secretary of State of Katherine Harris was essentially allowed to single-handily decide who won between Republican George W. Bush and Al Gore. Harris was a Republican, and Bush won, despite more Americans in the country voting for Al Gore. This is in no way to say that either Bush winning or Gore winning was the "correct" choice, only that our system sucks, if it can ever come down to one party-affiliated person getting to choose who wins in a country of over three hundred million people. In your own state, it is highly likely that a party-appointed secretary of state or lieutenant governor is the primary overseer of all your elections, from dog catcher to congressional representatives to president. It would be a huge improvement to our system, if every state refused to allow this person to be a member of a political party and forced oversight into nonpartisan and objective hands.

So what can you do? The following...

1) Go to Change.org to start a petition (or a citizen's

initiative if your state allows) for removing election and voting processes in your state from either party's control, and toward nonpartisan oversight. They have a free online petition generator which will not only allow you to easily draft the petition, but also get momentum by sending it out over social media prior to delivering it to your chosen governmental recipients. Demand that whoever oversees your state's elections, whether secretary of state or lieutenant governor, renounce any party affiliation, or move election oversight from their control to a nonpartisan committee.

2) Sign up at independ.me to stay informed of great new independent resources and to know when future updates to this book are released.

Key Section Takeaways

No official with any election oversight capabilities should be allowed to remain a member of any group trying to win those elections.

States B3: *End Preferential Treatment for Political Parties (Tax Exemption, Special Postage, Voter Rolls) in Your State*

In most states the two major political parties enjoy preferential treatment on taxes and costs associated with running campaigns. These advantages can sometimes include discounted postage rates for mail advertising and cheaper rates for accessing voter roll information in order to target their intended supporters. It may not seem like a big deal, but in some areas, this can make it cost-prohibitive for any unrecognized third parties or independents to compete.

So what can you do? The following...

1) Research for your particular state if the Republicans or Democrats receive any special treatment, including cheaper taxes, postage, or fees to access voter information. Then go to Change.org to start a petition (or citizen's initiative if your state allows) to stop these unfair advantages which help keep them in power.

Key Section Takeaways

Try to find out about the preferential treatment Republicans and Democrats are given in your own area and fight to end it

Chapter Eight

Keeping our Freedoms Free

This book is designed as a nonpartisan blueprint for independents to make systematic reform, rather than to promote specific political causes. In reality, however, it is impossible to always and completely separate the system's functioning from its results. Some issues fall into preexisting political platforms for either the right or left, but their success or failure will directly support or diminish the improved democracy as we are outlining here. In this chapter we list two very broad issues you should consider supporting, whether their champions come from the right, left, or anywhere else: protecting the First and Fourth amendments to the Constitution.

If you'd like a more in-depth look at this book's ideology, go to the chapter on "A Possible New Political Ideology For You," but suffice to say, it primarily supports policies that try to ensure ALL American citizens can equally exercise their free will. If Americans aren't free, none of the other stuff is possible or matters. Pretty straightforward, right? As such, we encourage any independents to think about supporting candidates, platforms, and organizations that resonate with supporting your First and Fourth amendment rights. Of course, first and foremost, you should always learn about the issues for yourself and make up your own mind what you will support. But, bottom line, if we don't keep vigilant on protecting our rights from government, history shows we will most likely have them taken away. Just being able to discuss why it's important with your friends and family will make a huge difference. The Constitution was written to protect YOUR power, not the government's ability to control you.

Fighting for the First Amendment

Possibly the most important rights you are guaranteed in the Constitution are those listed in the First Amendment, which spells out the protection each of us has to speak as we choose and practice any religion we wish (or even none at all), along with freedom of the press, and freedom of assembly, including political discussions and protests.

It reads: "*Congress shall make no law respecting an establishment of religion, or prohibiting the free exercise thereof; or abridging the freedom of speech, or of the press; or the right of the people peaceably to assemble, and to petition the Government for a redress of grievances.*"

All in all, the rights protected within the First Amendment are often lumped together under the term "free speech," and it is incredibly important to keeping our democracy alive. As George Washington warned, "*If the freedom of speech is taken away, then dumb and silent we may be led, like sheep to the slaughter.*"

Unfortunately, as time goes on with generations of Americans knowing no threats to their freedom of speech, the idea of actively protecting it has possibly diminished in importance. In modern America, there has even recently been a progressive movement to try to control "hate speech," or put another way, to actually limit particular people's free speech. This trend is dangerously misguided, even if it is well intended.

As attorney Gabe Rottman explains in an *American Civil Liberties Union* article: "once you give the government the ability to silence unpopular speech, no one is safe. Once you start playing favorites with the protections of the First Amendment, you put yourself at the mercy of shifting political whims. Free speech only for some translates directly into free speech for none."

In reality, if you truly understand the important of the

First Amendment to our personal freedoms and democracy, you understand there is no such thing as "hate speech," at least not in any way that should be legally restricted.

What does the publicly praying religious group have in common with the marching gay group? And the dumbass Fox News anchor with the ridiculous MSNBC host? They're all guaranteed their ability to think their thoughts and voice their ideas because of the First Amendment and free speech. True, that means idiots, lunatics, and evil people get to spout off, but that's okay. Rather than dangerously trying to regulate speech through laws, we should all just be using our own freedom of speech to rationally argue against the hateful, the crazy, and the ignorant. Bad ideas can only truly be defeated in public debate, not through laws attempting to shut them up. Speech that might make you uncomfortable, is actually the price of making sure all our freedoms are respected.

The First Amendment is the most powerful of all the "checks and balances" necessary to keep democracy alive for us all, and it is incredibly dangerous to take away any of our collective rights in the misguided hope of regulating our way to a verbal utopia. There has never been a successful dictator that has not curtailed their people's freedom of speech, because in the history of the world there has never been a tyrannical government able to stay in power when freedom of speech was actually present. The bottom line is you should be fighting to protect our freedom of speech in all cases, without exception, or as George Washington warned above, our democracy won't exist without it.

As such, you might want to consider supporting groups that fight to protect free speech and related First Amendment rights. One of the better ones is the *First Amendment Coalition* (firstamendmentcoalition.org), which has successfully defended First Amendment rights in several court cases, and is dedicated to protecting everyone's right to free speech, even offering free legal counsel in some cases to those whose rights have been violated. Additionally, the *Freedom Forum Institute* (freedomforuminstitute.org) makes free speech and First Amendment rights a focal point of their work, and may be worthy of your interest or support. Last, but certainly not least, is the powerful *American Civil Liberties Union* (aclu.org), which often draws criticism from extremists for their insistence on fighting for everyone's rights to free speech, even deplorable groups. Almost all successful free speech federal court cases since the twentieth century have had ACLU assistance, so this is an extremely worthy group for you to support. You can go to any of their websites to learn more and maybe sign up.

Anything you can do to understand on a deeper level, discuss, and fight for First Amendment causes, will absolutely serve to help our country. As long as free speech is still present, we'll always have a fighting chance to end the two-party's corruption, inequality, and dysfunction, while also intelligently debating ideas rather than resorting to belligerent polarization.

Fighting for the Fourth Amendment

The Fourth Amendment to the Constitution is arguably second only in importance to the First for keeping our democracy viable. The Fourth Amendment reads: "*The right of the people to be secure in their persons, houses, papers, and effects, against unreasonable searches and seizures, shall not be violated, and no Warrants shall issue, but upon probable cause, supported by Oath or affirmation, and particularly describing the place to be searched, and the persons or things to be seized.*"

It is often summarized as your "right to privacy" and is closely tied to the idea of popular sovereignty, the concept that you and your things are inherently yours, not to be messed with by the government, or anyone else, unless there is legal justification to do so. Unfortunately, this right is quickly eroding in the United States because of changes to technology as well as lax interpretations by law enforcement to unjustly seize people's money and possession without any evidence of a crime. Even more frightening, some in government are actively attempting to reduce your protections even further. There have been several pieces of legislation passed since 2001 that are being used for clear encroachments on your Constitutional right of privacy, such as *FISA*, the *Patriot Act*, and the *USA Freedom Act*.

Where to draw the line between threats of terrorism, privacy, and technological change are difficult issues, but the current lack of public accountability for these law's uses is setting a dangerous precedent for what the president and executive agencies, such as the Justice Department, National Security Agency, Central Intelligence Agency, and Internal Revenue Service, can do to you. You can read a detailed breakdown on issues with each of these laws in Paul Bischoff's 2018 article, "A Breakdown of the Patriot Act, the Freedom Act, and FISA," for *Comparitech*.

A frightening side effect of ongoing twenty-first-century technological advancements means they have vastly more power to infringe, often without you knowing. If you haven't watched the 2014 documentary about Edward Snowden, *CitizenFour*, it would probably be good to do so. And keep in mind, when Snowden revealed this information, the government had been flatly denying they were doing it, so, what could they be lying about now? Some privacy advocates speculate the government might already be keeping a record of pretty much all your travels, communications, and online searches, without ever needing a warrant or even suspicion of a crime, simply to have the information in case you ever do act in a way someone at the government doesn't like. The technology exists, so why wouldn't they? If this doesn't scare you, you're probably just preferring to hope it can't be true, rather than actually thinking about it.

Jen Briney's *Congressional Dish* has another fascinating podcast episode (Episode 98) that can give you some frightening details on the passage of the *USA Freedom Act*. Suffice to say, these laws are being used unjustly far more often against American citizens than any of the terrorists they were purportedly passed for. As an October 2018 *Washington Post* article reported, decades after its inception, the *Patriot Act* had actually been used in over fifteen hundred drug-related court cases, but only fifteen times against terrorists. As of 2014, it had been used over eleven thousand times for arguably unconstitutional sneak-and-peek warrant requests (whereby law officers were allowed to break into personal residences and property to gather evidence without the owners being informed) against US citizens, with only fifty-one of these incidents related to terrorism. Bottomline, these laws are often not actually being used for their stated purpose of combatting foreign terrorism, but are primarily being used against American citizens.

Slowly eroding your Fourth Amendment protections

over the past two decades is definitely not protecting you from any two-party oligarchs wanting to solidify their power, so we need to fight against it. As Thomas Paine said, "*It is the duty of the patriot to protect his country from its government.*" If we just accept these violations of privacy and property rights by the government it continues to set awful precedents. Even our own personal habits with technology can be extremely dangerous to our democracy.

The great legal scholar and privacy advocate Jeffrey Rosen at ConstitutionCenter.org has a seven-minute video explaining the key issues in your right to privacy and technology. As Mr. Rosen elucidates, the core concern is that as technology advances, it makes language in the Fourth Amendment harder to apply to modern real-world concerns. The amendment's authors in colonial America could not have possibly envisioned the internet and cell phones, so did not anticipate your need to protect your privacy beyond your "persons, houses, papers, and effects," yet they obviously wanted us to have these protections in any way they could understand. Unless we fight back against the government, as they continue to use the three laws mentioned above (and others) as justification to broaden their ability to eavesdrop on you, compile information on you regardless of getting a warrant, and possibly seize your property without your being convicted of any crime, we are passively eroding our own rights. We must be pointing out the *unreasonable*ness of their actions, or we are allowing the legal precedent to be set that it can continue to happen.

It's therefore crucial that we not only support those fighting against the government using these three laws to erode our Fourth Amendment rights, but also take on personal responsibility of protecting our privacy more in cell phone and internet communications. If we take steps to fight the encroachment, and protect our privacy even within new technology, then the courts have no option other than to see any efforts to invade this as "unreasonable," as is described in the Constitution.

Some of the simpler things you can do to fight for your Fourth Amendment rights are encrypting your online communication through virtual proxy networks (VPNs), using encrypted email providers, choosing non-tracking internet browsers like Duckduckgo and Tor, as well as turning off cell phone GPS and data gathering from apps when not in use. There are even easy-to-install smartphone apps like Signal and What'sApp that will even automatically encrypt all data, including phone calls, between you and other users. The important thing is not to give in to feeling overwhelmed by the complexity of technology, but take whatever steps you can to protect your privacy.

Additionally, you can also use and support the efforts of the *Electronic Frontier Foundation* (eff.org), the *Fourth Amendment Advisory Committee* (fourthadvisory.org), and the *National Association of Criminal Defense Lawyers* (nacdl.org), in their efforts to protect the Fourth Amendment for all. As always, in regards to issues of citizen's rights against the government, the ACLU is again worthy of knowing and supporting, as well as an amazing law group called the *Institute for Justice* (ij.org) that will often fight the government for people needing their civil rights protected. Also, although this book does not intend to completely endorse any particular politician, within the realm of privacy concerns, Senator Rand Paul (Republican) and Representative Tulsi Gabbard (Democrat) appear worthy of your consideration for support and assistance. Their often solitary efforts to protect American privacy against the rest of government could use help, even if it is through you just badgering your own representatives to give them a hand. Additionally, there are currently at least two bills in the 116th Congress which might be worth your support depending on what their final wording turns out to be: Senator John Kennedy's *S 806 Own Your Own Data Act,* and Senator Amy Klobuchar's *S 189 Privacy Protection and Consumer Rights Act.*

Last, fighting for your rights on your individual state's level is often faster and more productive than waiting on the federal government to change. You could use California's recent 2018 legislation to ensure online privacy as an example to demand your state legislature does the same. You can even use the ACLU's website to find the status of internet privacy legislation for your individual state. This is an incredibly important issue for you to understand, talk about, and fight for. If we let the Fourth Amendment disappear, our freedom will disappear with it.

Chapter Nine

Decentralizing Power Through Technology, and Other Cool Ideas

The ideas presented in this chapter are simply brought up as food for thought in areas we could collectively explore going forward. They largely involve either technological invention, or simply a new way of looking at things, which could potentially help revamp our system into one that fosters more independent and nuanced decision making. Decentralizing power as much as is functionally possible will always be the best way to keep government from being corrupted, lessen two-party control, and protect popular sovereignty for every American.

Cool Idea 1: *Blockchain Voting*

The mechanics of America's system for voting is woefully inadequate, highly susceptible to manipulation from both inside and outside the country. If you want to learn some horrifying facts about how bad our current voting machine system actually is, listen to computer security expert Stephen Spoonamore via youtube give the details to ABC News back in 2012. As he was warning back then, most people don't realize that almost all voting machines currently in use around the country are controlled by only a few private companies, all heavily associated with one of the two controlling political parties, and not legally required to have any oversight regarding the vote tallies they claim to produce. Not only are we simply supposed to take the word of these private companies that they are accurately and honestly providing vote totals, but even if they weren't purposely trying to throw elections in one direction or another, their security is currently laughable. In 2018 and 2019 it became clear that the Russians already hacked into a great deal of voting systems around the country. You can also even watch a 2018 PBS news video of an eleven-year-old hacking into a Florida voting machine in under ten minutes to alter vote totals, or watch an equally disturbing 2006 HBO documentary called (hackingdemocracy.com) *Hacking Democracy.*

Though the companies controlling the voting machines have kept changing names over the past ten years, it turns out its still actually mostly all the same people, same machines, and same lack of oversight or rules for them. Even if these private companies, without any oversight or accountability were working with the absolute best of intentions, which is extremely doubtful, the way the system is structured, means it is almost inevitable that some other group, including foreign powers like Russia, will be able to hack in and completely alter the results of major American elections in the very near future... if they haven't already done so. At a minimum, it allows ample ability for either of the Republicans or Democrats to manipulate vote totals without the public ever knowing about it, because there is currently not even any way to audit their results.

First and foremost, you might want to support one of the election reform bills that have been introduced to 116th Congress that promote at least having some sort of paper ballot check/audit system for electronic vote totals. One of the better ones might be Democrat Zoe Lofgren's *HR 2722 SAFE Act*.

More exciting over the long-term though, would be the solution of internet voting through blockchain technology. It actually wouldn't be that difficult to implement. Block-chain would essentially allow everyone to publicly verify vote total accuracy instead of a few "gatekeepers." To learn more details about the way blockchain technology works in under two minutes watch *Institute for the Future's* 2016 video on youtube. When you think about it, it's kind of amazing that most banking is now done online, yet online voting is basically nonexistent. We can send all our money around the internet every single day with few problems, but we can't safely tally votes once every couple of years? Come on.

Any democracy can only ever be as functional and legitimate as the votes that give it authority, so making ours as ideal as possible is pretty damn important. And the thing is, the blockchain technology necessary to make internet voting work is already here, we just need to implement it. It will even save money for the American people, while increasing security, transparency, and privacy of the voting system, and increasing voter turnout by making voting from home a reality.

In its simplest explanation, blockchain can now give us the ability to have everyone verify vote totals, rather than some two-party sponsored individuals in a back room somewhere. We would no longer need to rely on privately controlled machines that can be manipulated by their owners or hacked by malicious groups. It would be incredibly easy to have a system whereby anyone with a smartphone or internet access could securely and privately vote, absolutely ensuring that their, and all other votes, are counted accurately. The real concern, like is a trend throughout American political problems, is that corrupted individuals and groups want to keep the flawed status quo so they can continue manipulating it to their advantage rather than allowing improvements.

Luckily, a group called *Follow My Vote* (followmyvote.com) is already hard at work on the problem and making good headway, as well as a second organization named *NetVote* (verifiedvoting.com). All either of them need is your support, either by donating or spreading the word of what the problem and solution is. From their website, *Follow My Vote* explains: "Using this advanced technology we will be able to gain transparency into our elections, without compromising voter privacy, and have a way to mathematically proving that election results are accurate. Also, at the voter's request, there would even be a way to allow a voter to cast their vote online in an election and follow their vote into the ballot box to ensure that their vote was safely and securely stored without being changed or altered in any way."

Moving all of American voting to internet-based blockchain will improve everything from security to transparency to voter turnout to election costs. And, if we don't make this change in the near future, it is very likely there will eventually be some sort of nefarious election interference that pushes us toward a Constitutional crisis, whether from within the country or without, and possibly an unrecoverable loss of legitimacy in our election processes and government.

Cool Idea 2: *Incentivized Voting*

It has recently been theorized that part of America's polarization problem could be mitigated by increasing voter turnout. The theory goes that if only more Americans would vote (only about 50 percent of eligible voters currently do) then the extremist bases of the two parties would be less important, and force both Republicans and Democrats toward moderation to win the votes of the bulk of citizens. Looking at countries where voting is legally required, like Australia (where around 90 percent of those eligible consistently vote), it shows that there is probably validity to this theory.

As the *Huffington Post* explains about the mandatory Australian voting system: "The original intent, or one of the arguments, for compulsory voting was that it would make elections about policy. We'd stop pleading for people to vote and just talk about policy. You wouldn't have to spend all your time with a get-out-the-vote effort. Now we do have campaigns about policy. It's not just trying to appeal to a particular sector to vote. You appeal to everybody. The parties have gotten good at appealing to the middle voter." This system seems to achieve its goals, consistently forcing more Australians to pay attention to politics, and thereby forcing more would-be Australian politicians to cater to the more moderate middle voters.

However, that said, compulsory voting ain't gonna work in America, and this book won't ever support the idea of making voting legally required here. Making a law requiring all Americans to vote is simply, well, un-American. The idea of popular sovereignty, and its closely associated attribute of individual freewill, would absolutely be reduced through a law forcing people to participate in the election process. However, there is potentially a way to get the best of both worlds by getting many more voters involved without legally forcing them to do so: financially incentivized voting.

Instead of making it illegal and punishable if you don't vote, America could try giving a tax deduction to all those who do vote. Innovative thinkers such as Yale's Stephen Carter have been suggesting this idea for a few years now. This would provide a motivation to get more people engaged, while still allowing people freewill to not participate if they so choose. Initially, some people against this idea will probably say that it would be logistically hard to implement, but this is simply not true if we were to move to the internet-based blockchain voting system mentioned earlier. Additionally, by increasing voter turnout we would thereby lessen political polarization as Australia has seen, and would maybe allow us to try an even more radical idea: raising voter knowledge in tandem with the voting numbers.

Sadly, increasing voter turnout has also become a right vs left issue in modern America, with Republicans largely fighting for stricter requirements to reduce numbers and raise voter "quality," and Democrats fighting for lower requirements to increase overall numbers no matter how disengaged the populous. Like most things in American politics though, it seems the obvious answer is that we want both. And it could be done.

What if in order to qualify to vote you had to pass a very basic ten-question, open-book, multiple-choice exam on the Constitution? No one would have to vote if they didn't want to, but if you were an adult and passed the exam, you would be eligible to vote and receive your tax deduction. The tax incentive would encourage more people to vote, while the very basic quiz would serve as a buffer that people at least had to somewhat think about what they were voting for before trying to do so. Obviously, some people are immediately going to have a problem with this idea and claim that it will somehow be used for voter suppression against certain classes or groups of people, but this doesn't have to be true. Through today's existing technology we could ensure the *Voting Rights Act* of 1965 is not violated, or any other concerns.

With the internet blockchain voting described above, the ten questions could be asked in the comfort of anyone's home, the same as they would securely vote from. There could even still be public voting centers available for those without internet access. The questions could be created by a nonpartisan groups of scholars, designed to not "stump" anyone, but simply encouraging a basic understanding of the Constitution. The quiz could even be open-book, with anyone allowed to read the Constitution as they take it, or even ask their friends and family for the answers. We even have the technology now so that people who cannot read or not speak English could have the questions and the Constitution itself read to them in their own language. In actuality, the idea would not really be to "fail" anyone, but simply give the average person a catalyst and reference point for starting individual thought and discussion about who they should vote for. It could even be possible that this system would actually help educate some people whom the school system has let down in regards to basic civics.

The reality is that we easily have the technology to do it, and if you leave polarized talking points behind, there is no reason why we shouldn't encourage as many politically educated Americans to vote as is possible. Hell, for those who don't feel the Constitutional quiz is fair, we could even still allow them to opt out to vote the same way as we do now, just forgoing their tax deduction. Isn't it about time to start thinking outside the box for real improvements?

Cool Idea 3: *Creating Governmental Artificial Intelligence*

Is it time to start letting computers replace some of our governmental leaders or processes? Granted, nobody wants some Terminator-scenario with a bunch of metallic bastards blasting us in the face with ray guns, but it seems like there might be some reasonable function for intelligent computing in our government going forward. In fact, the technology of artificial intelligence is so imminent to being a part of our lives, the best way to avoid a doomsday scenario up ahead is to start more discussion now about how it should be used.

There are many ideas of what artificial intelligence in government could look like, some of them pretty sci-fi compared to our current state. On one extreme, picture altruistic and brilliant robots replacing all of our loser politicians, or maybe some sort of giant mainframe dictating all of our government processes from a dark room atop a tower like the Wizard of Oz. Obviously, this type of scenario is a far ways off, and is probably the exact circumstance where we would be exterminated, once the AI logically determines we'd all be better off if there were just less of us. There are, however, some much more mundane and quickly achievable scenarios for implementing artificial intelligence in our government to make things more functional and transparent. If done correctly, it could reduce governmental bureaucracy and eliminate redundant laws and regulatory agencies, while increasing that all-important popular sovereignty for the average American citizen. And maybe we don't even have to get hunted by robot-dogs!

There is even a governmental agency called *The Network and Information Technology Research and Development Program* (nitrd.gov) apparently already created to deal with integrating AI into government. Now, don't lose any sleep over the fact that the governmental program apparently in charge of implementing AI has a website that looks like it was last updated in the 90s, because luckily, there appear to be some brilliant geeks outside of government who are also working on this. *The Center for Public Impact* (centerforpublicimpact.org) is putting a lot of thought and effort into trying to create a blueprint for governments around the world to start integrating AI. They've even created a detailed report about it, *How to Make AI Work for Government and People*, if you'd like to check it out.

Most likely, in the near future any aggressive implementation of AI and internet-based solutions to government will still largely deal with making the process and function of government more efficient, rather than replacing or trying to improve the actual decision-making. A good example America could use as inspiration for initial change would be the country of Estonia (e-estonia.com), which over the last few years has made radical changes to become the world's leader for technology enhancing government. What is probably most important at this time is in getting laypeople involved in the discussion of how artificial intelligence could most positively be used in government. Like with any software or hardware, AI will only be good for us if it is programmed with the correct goals in mind. We suggest that as AI begins to merge with governments around the world, protocols should be set up from the beginning to ensure it is working to enhance popular sovereignty, or gross national happiness like in Bhutan, or some other standard that most all people can agree upon. If we don't spread the word and start debating what AI's governmental goals should be now, we do run the risk of it becoming yet another, even more powerful tool, for the corrupt to protect their dictatorial power. Or maybe Skynet killing us all with their Terminators.

Cool Idea 4: *Speaking of Technology, Let's Help Congress' Old Idiots Keep Up*

Congress can't make effective laws to deal with increasingly rapid technological changes if they're so out of step they don't even understand what the technology is. Many people were more than a little bit horrified at how ignorant to recent technological changes most of Congress appeared when Facebook CEO Mark Zuckerberg publicly testified before them.

According to a 2019 *Politico* article suggesting House reforms: "From its inadequate constituent service software, to its hackable communications systems, to the staggering lack of technology experts available to advise members on some of the fastest-moving and most important policy issues they face, the House needs a major update."

The article, written by members of Legbranch.org (a nonprofit attempting to reform Congress to function better) goes on to suggest that Congress could be helped by reinstating the defunct *Office of Technology Assessment*. The nonpartisan office used to provide reports to Congress on technological changes so that they could understand them, but the office was closed under Newt Gingrich budget-cutting efforts in the 1990s. With the impact of things like artificial intelligence, biochemical warfare, internet privacy, and nanotechnology only increasing in importance and risk from here forward, it seems like reviving, or creating something similar to, the *Office of Technology Assessment* is pretty damn important. If Congress has a hard time understanding Facebook, are we really going to have any hope of them grasping virtual reality, artificial intelligence and molecular-sized robots? And as Deepfake videos become more prevalent, will people in Congress even know what's real? Scary shit.

Cool Idea 5: *Peaceful Political Terrorism and Constitutional Conventions*

Moving away from technology toward some more pedestrian, yet still exciting ways of thinking, Professor Lawrence Lessig has some unique ideas of how to radically change things in his book *Republic, Lost*. Possibly two more interesting ideas are for the encouragement of "peaceful political terrorists" and for a grassroots movement toward calling for a general constitutional convention.

In regards to "peaceful political terrorism," Lessig points out that there is a loophole in the Constitution that allows anyone residing in a particular state to run for multiple House of Representative seats within that state at the same time. His idea would basically be for well-known, nonpolitical individuals across the country to run for any and all closely battled congressional districts in their state on one-issue platforms, with a guarantee that they would decline the office or retire after they won and resolved the issue they ran on. As Lessig sees financial corruption as the core problem for America's government, he encourages these "peaceful terrorists" to make their single issue be about financial reform, yet the reality is that this issue could be any of the reform concerns listed in this book. The way it would basically work is having someone with at least some name recognition—think an actor, sports star, or well-known businessman—pulling lots of votes away from both Republicans and Democrats in closely fought districts, until at least one of them publicly addresses their concern. Even if the "peaceful terrorist" doesn't win a single race, they will force attention to that chosen issue, and probably force those on both the right and left toward addressing it. If the "peaceful terrorist" did end up winning, then it would be ideal for them to fulfill their obligation to enact the change they ran on, quitting as soon as it was achieved. Obviously, this plan requires selfless individuals who are more concerned with changing the system than increasing their own power, but possibly these people do exist and would respond well to this idea.

In a different fashion, grassroots efforts to call for an open-ended constitutional convention would also serve as a serious threat to the political establishment. Article V of the Constitution explains that it would currently take only thirty-four states demanding a constitutional convention to be convened wherein any and all potential amendments to the Constitution could be debated and voted on for immediate implementation. Lessig supports the idea of a nationwide grassroots movement beginning toward this end, without worrying too much about the specifics of exactly what issues it would address, or what amendments would be voted on. Arguing over all the details could mean forever prevent it from happening, and professor Lessig thinks anything and everything should just be assumed to be fair game for debate so long as we can just get the convention approved.

Granted, there is a bit of danger in this strategy of some extremists hijacking the cause, but it is probably less dangerous than allowing the status quo to continue unchecked. Lessig seems to believe in trusting in the law of large numbers that as long as there are enough people aware and involved in a constitutional convention, any changes made to the Constitution would be reasonable ones. Like with the earlier idea though, just the grassroots effort itself might cause politicians on the right and left to address different concerns. And if a constitutional convention were called for the first time since the founding of our country, it would not be something to fear, but would actually be the most American thing to happen for democracy since 1776. Heck, isn't it time to shake stuff up... why not start recruiting peaceful political terrorists and calling for a constitutional convention in your own state right now? It'd be more entertaining than watching Netflix.

Cool Idea 6: *Suing the Two Parties for Anti-Trust Behavior*

As mentioned earlier in this book, Michael Porter and Katherine Gehl authored a Harvard study on how a true lack of competition to Republicans and Democrats is hurting all of American governance. To get great insight on both their findings and solutions, listen to their interview on the *Freakonomics* podcast, episode 356. In this interview, Gehl and Porter use an example of the Republicans and Democrats effectively being like Coke and Pepsi. They are tacitly rivals to each other, but only in an agreed upon, limited way that increases both of their chances of remaining as the only two viable alternatives for any consumers (voters) and always keeping barriers of entry impossibly high to any other potential rivals. Even worse than Coke and Pepsi, however, the Republicans and Democrats are arguably colluding more explicitly to create and keep a monopoly over the political marketplace. Gehl and Porter suggest suing the Republican and Democratic parties based on anti-trust statutes and forcing them to break up their monopoly.

It is beyond the scope of this book to determine if there could be a legally viable lawsuit, either federally or within any state statues, for this kind of action, but it's probably worth looking into. Much like the ideas suggested in section 4, this threat, if legitimate, could force some positive changes within the two major parties. And if a lawsuit were actually won proving that the Republicans and Democrats are acting as a monopoly, forcing them to break themselves up, it could be a hugely positive step toward ensuring there would forever be more political choice. We're looking at you, bored attorneys who want to make a name for yourselves.

Cool Idea 7: *Require Media to Balance Political Coverage Again, And Create a Game Plan for Fighting Biased Bullshit*

Almost all mainstream media at this point has become biased for either the political right or left, and is thereby not helping the polarization problems engulfing our country. Fighting for re-instituting something akin to the *Federal Communication Commission*'s "Fairness Doctrine" regarding media political coverage could go a long way toward helping things. Up until 1987, the FEC required that all public media give equal and balanced coverage to all political opinion. Since that time the requirement has been removed. Probably not coincidentally, since around that same time America has seen the rise of blatantly biased talk radio, and most all of the mainstream news outlets have been hijacked by the political agendas of either the Republicans or Democrats to one degree or another. In fact, compared to the 1970s when fully two-thirds of Americans said they had faith that the mainstream news was offering balanced and factual political coverage, only 30 percent of Americans felt that way in 2016. Lack of trust in mainstream media has led people to more and more rely on internet-sourced news, which inherently has even more potential for being biased, and in many cases, outright propaganda, either from a political group in the US, or outside it.

If you really want to get a grasp of how serious the issue of not knowing who a trustworthy source of information will soon become, check out the May 2019 completely fake, computer-generated monologue of what appears to sound exactly like podcaster Joe Rogan from a company called Dessa. Their example is only audio, but should be troubling to anyone who thinks about the impact of easily accessible technology to convincingly make it sound like anyone is saying anything. And video, possibly even more damaging, is not far behind. As Bernhard Warner reports in his June 12th, 2019 fortune.com article Deepfake Video of Mark Zuckerberg Goes Viral on Eve of House A.I. Hearing, the ability for videos to be created of well-know individuals like Nancy Pelosi and Mark Zuckerberg saying and doing things they've never said or done is rapidly increasing. Watch the deep fake Zuckerberg video online, and then consider the potential ramifications of a completely fake video of a political leader like Donald Trump or Vladimir Putin announcing nuclear strikes or chemical attacks online. Sure, it would hopefully eventually be found out as fake, but is there a chance WWIII could be started before it did? If we don't start to develop some standards now, imagine a very near future whereby you will not even be able to trust what you see or hear on your computer or television ever happened at all, let alone that it is being basely spun in one political direction or the other. Or just as bad, things get so confusing that otherwise rational people start to jump on a fear-based bandwagon of the government taking away their free speech.

Somehow re-establishing America's trust in unbiased, factual news and sources of information well be crucial to protecting a peaceful society going forward. It can't be done accurately though with only corrupt Republicans and Democrats pulling all the strings. There are some interesting legislative proposals to deal with the deep fake issue in the 116th Congress, but these should be examined extremely closely before implementing into law. A couple that might deserve to be look at are Senator Rob Portman's *s 2065 Deepfake Report Act* and Senator Josh Hawley's *S 2314* bill to prohibit social media from tricking us. Again though, in issues of rapid technological advancement, we need to make sure the solution does not actually become the poison through threatening the First Amendment.

First and foremost this book always believes free speech should be prioritized over other concerns, so it seems like there could be public standard agreed upon for what is considered ethical and factual reporting, while avoiding laws that potentially restrict free speech. Maybe by providing incentives to media organizations that hold themselves to a true standard of political objectivity? Debating the particulars of how this would work, and how to protect ourselves from biased reporting and completely deep fake news as technology rapidly advances are beyond the current scope of this book, but it would be a benefit for people to start thinking and talking about it now.

Finland might serve as example for some of the solution. As a 2019 CNN video shows they have been setting up public classes on how to spot fake news for several years. Google "Finland fake news classes" to see videos of what they are doing with apparent good results. Citizens need to have reasonable faith that their information is not corrupted by either the government in power, some group trying to obtain power, or even a foreign power. This is a tricky subject to navigate, but crucial as barriers to mass communication continue to drop around the world.

How do we help to increase the free flow of information, while at the same time helping to ensure people know who to trust? The best solution is probably some sort of government standard (not law) being advised, education (like Finland), and the free market rising to combat bad technology with good. Let's try to figure it out... quickly.

Cool Idea 8: *Understand and Use Citizen's Initiatives More Aggressively (And Even Write Your Own Laws)*

So did you know there is actually a way for you to completely circumvent your state legislature if you don't like what they are doing? As in, you, a single individual, can actually orchestrate getting a law passed or repealed in 24 states regardless of what elected politicians want. Given that state laws are generally in control of their own election and political finance regulations, as well as numerous other crucial checks to federal power, this is a hugely powerful tool for you to understand and implement when necessary.

Depending on the particular state, Citizen's Initiatives may be called a popular initiative, ballot initiative, or a few other names, but they are all essentially the same process of your gathering enough of your fellow citizen's signatures to place a proposed law on the ballot for general rejection or acceptance by popular vote. You can make this proposal very general, or even use something like ncls.org's bill drafting manual to write out a law ready for submission to your state or national Congress. You can find more details about the citizen's initiative process in your state at ballotpedia.org/ ballot_initiative , but they all largely follow the same simple procedure... 1) create a law you want passed, or identify one you want repealed, 2) go throughout your community to get enough signature support to meet your state's requirement, and 3) once it is on the ballot try to get as many people as you can to vote for your change. Change org is great place to start something like this as it has easy to use templates and ways to blast your petition out to everyone in your social media groups.

The National Conference of State Legislatures (ncls.org) has some excellent information for individual states. Even if you don't end up starting one today, this powerful resource is important to understand for future political battles, and a big weapon any grassroots political movement.

Cool Idea 9: *If You Want Something Easy, Just Sign Up For These Top 4 Political Reform Groups*

Although you're spending the time to read part or all of this book, maybe you're now just wondering what the simplest, most impactful, steps are for you to take. We'd suggest it's in signing up for the four robust groups below. Each has a slightly unique, take on what needs to be done, and lending your support to any is a simple net positive to our country.

Represent Us (represent.us) Possibly the most vibrant, well thought out, and organized group pushing for corrections to America's core political problems. You should go on their website to watch the Jennifer Lawrence hosted video "Unbreaking America," and then consider joining their extremely strategic grassroots push to enact the *American Anti-Corruption Act* on your local level.

Fair Vote (fairvote.org) Probably the smartest, and maybe longest acting, electoral reform organization, their intelligent work perpetually points to our current governmental issues and solutions for it. Sign up for the newsletter, and see how you can help.

No Labels (nolabels.org) Making genuine headway in Washington, No Labels is provide structural, policy and issues solutions for ending polarization in our country. It's a positive message and a great idea, and you can even sign up to become one of their grassroots "Ambassadors" to help spread the message.

SAM (joinsam.org) Describing itself as a new "political party," it nonetheless appears laser-focused on achieving the same goals as outlined in this book, breaking two party corruption, and improving the structure of our democracy.

Cool Idea 10: *Stop Following Parties, and Start Following Socrates*

Ancient Greece actually invented democracy with America's founding fathers both inspired by, and drawing from, that first republic in their construction of ours. And the wisest man from that era, even arguably from all of history thus far, Socrates said, "*true knowledge is knowing you know nothing*."

Possibly the most impactful and positive thing you can actually do for our democracy is to emulate Socrates, by actually considering that you, yes you, are the problem with your own certainty, and maybe you don't know as much as you think you do. Maybe focus on making yourself better, before correcting others. Maybe proactively hold yourself accountable to the concepts of humility, reason, and empathy in discussions. Maybe realize that no matter how many degrees or instagram followers you've got, you're actually still a fucking idiot. Hey, don't get pissy, just referencing Socrates' point here... it's actually pretty much impossible for any of us to know permanent truth regarding anything, and the wisest thing we can all do is be a little more humble in our self-perceived "correctness."

A more detailed examination of a potential new political ideology for you is explored in Chapter Eleven, but suffice to say, you personally breaking "two-party thought" by no longer confidently parroting red or blue (or any other party for that matter) talking points, and committing to a deeper, nuanced examination of all sides in political issues, would be a huge help. Reactionary, binary thinking on issues is ripping America apart at its seams, even as it benefits most of those Republicans and Democrats in power. You overcoming this simplistic thinking, by listening first for things you can recognize and relate to in others, as well as focusing on common ground you can agree with in your political opposition, could be the most impactful thing you ever do in life. It's time to bring back reasonable, logical debate as a virtue, and challenge anyone blindly participating in supporting a party line.

You can learn more about concepts like the "Socratic Method" and logical debate on wikipedia, but even if that requires missing too much time away from America's Got Talent, or sharing dank cat memes, maybe just try this thought experiment for a while— whenever someone on "your political side" states something, consider that they might not have all the facts (i.e. doubt them), and when someone on the "other political side" says something, try to imagine what would have to of happened differently in your own life in order for you to actually agree with them (i.e. empathize). It's a practice in humility and understanding others, and it would go along great with promoting these additional concepts, instead of two-party thinking:

*Logical consistency in everyone's communication
*Personal ethics in yourself, but less judgment of others
*Reason and moderation as beneficial goals
*Rational debate being beneficial, and not getting personally offended by it

Because, again, as Socrates figured out long ago, we're all actually kind of stupid. But you can immediately become the smartest person in the room, if you're the one who realizes it.

Part Three

Resources, Tools, and New Ways of Thinking

"We must, indeed, all hang together, or most assuredly, we'll all hang separately."

—Benjamin Franklin

Chapter Ten

An Oversimplified History, and Explanation of, American Government

(And no, the below is not claiming to be exhaustively accurate or replace your high school history classes; it's just an attempt to give a very general idea of how America works.)

In 1776, the geographical region now known as The United States of America was still ruled by England. Sick of some rich idiot (the King of England) telling them what to do, a bunch of brilliant American badasses (the founding fathers) told him to piss off, winning a war against the greatest empire the world had ever then known to get their freedom. Those American badasses then created our democratic system of governance, which effectively started turning the tide from dictatorships and tyranny in the world, to governments based on equal votes for citizens and much fairer laws. The founding fathers wrote our Constitution to explain how American government is designed to work, by ensuring no single person, group or government ever had unjust control over other citizens. The Constitution is America's highest law, and the basis upon which all other laws must ascribe. It's pretty important, so if you haven't ever read it, you probably should in order to have a core understanding of government, law, and your own rights (it's in Appendix Three).

Written in the Constitution is that core principle that American government needs "checks and balances," or permanent divisions of power between our branches of government to function properly and avoid corruption. Above all, the founding fathers wanted to forever avoid the possibility of America falling into the control of another dictator, like a king, or some other small group of people. In a way, you could say the Constitution and it's Bill of Rights is trying to protect every citizen's inherent "popular sovereignty," or free will. They made sure to design the Constitution so that all governmental control would be continuously cycled among multitudes of citizens, with no single position of power ever able to act unilaterally.

The American federal government is therefore permanently divided into three branches, known as the legislative (Congress), the executive (the president), and the judicial (the Supreme Court). No branch is superior to the other, but each acts with realms of power and abilities unique to itself, and ideally serves to keep the others in check. Together, the three branches should work to create, enforce, and revise the laws of the country to be most beneficial to all of its citizens. From taxation to jails, to how and when wars are fought, laws are essentially the way a government enacts our collective will within society. All three branches of the federal government can therefore best be simplified as to what role they have in the American legal system. The legislative branch (Congress) creates the laws, the executive (president) makes sure the laws are properly enforced through directing the government's actions, and the judicial (court system) decides if the laws are fair and have been executed correctly. Additionally, each state has its own government, which has certain jurisdictions of influence as well.

All of these governmental entities are ideally supposed to function from the bottom up, with each American citizen's vote mattering equally in who populates these governmental roles, and thereby what their focus will be as they perform their duty. The overarching goal of America's democracy was arguably to have all government ran by popular sovereignty, meaning all imaginable rights and freedoms inherently exist in each citizen for all time, and any power given to the government is only temporarily loaned from each individual to achieve goals of the collective citizenry through elected government officials. That's a very important concept to remember, as it essentially means the government can only function in ways that all of us collectively approve of. We're in charge, not them. And political parties, like the Republicans and Democrats, were never mentioned in the Constitution, and have no mandated role in our political process.

In modern times however, the two-party system has started sucking the American dream from its people like stank-breathed vampires, while we increasingly try to kill each other over our ever-evaporating happiness. They've achieved this through several systemic changes to the government and election processes since around the 1970s. Again, this timeline isn't perfect, but is simply giving you an overview of ideas to start considering:

i) Starting in the 1970s, a combination of court decisions, congressional rule changes, and the creation of legislative "earmarks" by both the Republicans and Democrats, led to a dramatic explosion of lobbying money to politicians. This increased their own wealth and power in exchange for policy decisions. Additionally, the 1967 *Uniform Congressional District Act* forced all states to be single-member districts, which conveniently helped ensure only Republicans or Democrats stay in power. Unsurprisingly, as Republicans and Democrats started to become self-aware of their tenuous ability to work together and get rich, we begin our timeline of many of the rising negative issues for the American people listed in Chapter One.

ii) By the 1990s, as the Republicans and Democrats increased their collusion so much to essentially morph into "one party of money" from an overall policy standpoint on those most heavily lobbied issues (like banking, military, NRA, etc.). And like two rival superpowers stockpiling nuclear warheads without ever really fighting, the massive influx of lobbying money exponentially inflated the media-based campaign costs for Republican and Democrats to jostle top-tier power from each other, without either one ever being demoted to less than second place. Instead of attempting to solve problems, they hijacked mainstream media to enflame America's culture wars, so citizens would fight among themselves yet always feel compelled to still vote for one wing of their system. Media companies have gotten richer than every before through going along with it, disregarding their journalistic integrity along the way. The parties also instituted self-serving moves like closed primaries and rigging over 80 percent of congressional seats via gerrymandering to create "safe districts," thereby making middle-ground swing voters largely irrelevant. Naturally, overall dissatisfaction with government and your fellow countrymen quickly grew through this time period.

iii) Since the 2000s, government has become even less effective, as the two parties have found it even more financially beneficial to stay in a state of permanent gridlock over the most emotionally charged social issues like racial rights, gay marriage, and abortion. This is because the permanent gridlock on social issues allows for more extremist rhetoric to motivate both sides of the duopoly's most dedicated bases, which are far more dependable for votes and donations than moderates. Extremist rhetoric has become endemic, while government functionality for the average American has bottomed-out. Those uncaring "elites" pulling the strings in government and business continue to get richer and richer, while much of the citizenry has wearily become resigned to the most corrupt, disgusting, lunatics in the country as being our only choices for president and other positions of power

But we can change things, starting now. Every person

breaking out of the misguided cult-like thinking of Republican versus Democrat, and then understanding how the Constitution actually designed America to work, is our greatest inoculation against yet again blindly supporting another "lesser of two evils" politician who falsely promises you simple answers within a red or blue T-shirt. And it is the basic strategy for correcting most of America's ills, not only in government function, but the polarization sickening its people as well. Don't hate your neighbor, fire your representative.

The full Constitution is included in this book so that you can read it for yourself, but there's also a great one-minute Hip Hughes video on youtube explaining the basics of the Constitution (it's a one-minute video for god's sake, don't be lazy). Just like the founding fathers knew, division of power is the most effective way of keeping it from being corrupted, and your personal knowledge is the greatest blade for slicing through power's corruption. Watch the video, and then when you get a free thirty minutes, read the whole Constitution provided at the end of the book. And then finally, encourage someone else to do the same.

Chapter Eleven

A Possible New Political Ideology for You

It is time to discuss this book's proposed new political ideology for you, an ideology many may consider radical, reckless, or even absurd: "no ideology." Your conscious personal adoption of a "no ideology" ideology for politics could be a more beneficial change to our country than any other single action you can take.

A "no ideology' ideology would mean you actively focus on the near-term real-world results you wish to cultivate related to each political issue as it arises, rather than reflexively aligning with any specific party or group's overall agenda. It would mean no longer allowing yourself to lazily outsource your thinking to someone in a red, blue, or any other color T-shirt, but ruthlessly supporting all good ideas regardless of the team that generated it. It would probably mean you would still sometimes reluctantly make those necessary descents into the muck of real-world political party divisions, but only for as short a time as possible. Someone prescribing to a "no ideology" ideology would potentially vote "conservative," or "liberal," or Libertarian, or anything else for any one issue or person, but always be hesitant to hoist that group's particular banner for all concerns. You would be suspicious of easy answers and always try to look deeper with your own logic, rationalism, and morality to avoid hypocrisy. It might sometimes even be a counterintuitive and lonely path, but we'd argue the time is desperately ripe for its need and adoption. It would mean for you to truly start thinking independently.

We'd recommend you read Jerry Taylor's excellent 2018 article "*The Alternative to Ideology*," for a real world example of someone moving from party-driven politics toward independent thought. Taylor is president of the nonprofit Washington think tank Niskanen, which until recently was

Libertarian. Libertarians, although closely aligning with this book on many issues, can also become myopic and tribal in their thinking if you get enough of them together parroting the same sound bites. Taylor has now courageously taken his organization from any party affiliation toward true independence, and his article is an excellent argument on why this is the correct call for every individual, at least into the foreseeable future.

Taylor writes in regards to his decision: "(it) is an invitation for you to do likewise—to walk out of the 'clean and well-lit prison of one idea.' Ideology encourages dodgy reasoning due to what psychologists call 'motivated cognition' which is the act of deciding what you want to believe and using your reasoning power, with all its might, to get you there. Worse, it encourages fanaticism, disregard for social outcomes, and invites irresolvable philosophical disputes. It also threatens social pluralism—which is to say, it threatens freedom... The better alternative is not moral relativism. The better alternative is moderation, a commodity that is rapidly disappearing in political life, with dangerous consequences for the American republic."

Your adopting a "no ideology" ideology would therefore not mean being disengaged, but would instead be the purest sense of political independence, by trying to get the best real-world results regardless of what group those ideas originate from. Obviously, in its most extreme sense, "no ideology" is tricky to implement however, as no one can achieve a perfect state of staying above all political ideas, concepts, and positions while at the same time trying to enact good within those same political structures. You will still need something upon which to personally judge which are better and worse goals to achieve. Ideals that would return focus from party tag lines to those few philosophical north stars from which we can determine eternal positives to navigate our real-world paths.

So what are those guiding principles that you can potentially rely on above worn-out party labels, impotent political catchphrases, or strict self-interest? That is essentially up to you, but we'd suggest they might have something to do with the following.

- Ending corruption and dysfunction in government

- Increasing diversity of parties, people and power in government, in order to safeguard it from being abused.

- Reinvigorating that idea that morality and intelligence are not mutually exclusive in politics, and that binary thinking between right and left will always give us inadequate solutions.

And maybe, the extremely beneficial concept of "moderation" that Taylor mentions earlier. There are many good ideals, and we can't make the decision for you as to what is most important at what times when it comes to politics, but it might be important to remember there is no single one ideal that can work in all situations, all the time. This is arguably why prioritizing ideals about how the system itself works is so important, and is exactly why the Constitution is so brilliant.

The founding fathers knew life itself is inherently too complex for any one leader or group to adequately guide it for all for all time. It was a large reason why the founders fought for a democracy to begin with. There are now over three hundred million of us in a melting pot of incalculable ethnicities, cultures, beliefs, and experiences, so it is somewhat naive to believe we will all want the exact same things. In fact, a central error some modern conservative or liberal voters appears to be in believing there was ever "one America" to begin with, or can ever be just "one America" up ahead.

A popular current conservative rallying cry is "Make America Great Again" as if there was once a singular, white-male-dominated country in which everyone was pleased and thinking in lockstep. Fundamentally untrue. Equally flawed however, is the progressive liberal dream that a perfectly cohesive utopia is in our future up ahead, once forcibly hammered into place by the strong arm of an infallible federal government. Collin Woodward's book *American Nations* describes the vast populating of the American continent from roughly 1500 to 1800 by up to as many as eleven distinct cultural "nations," in opposition to the commonly portrayed historical meme that all of America was essentially formed by white, Protestant, English-descent Yankees. True, most of the founding fathers did come from one particular "nation," but this small percentage of gentleman was keenly aware of the hugely disparate makeup of nationalities, beliefs, and motivations they were trying to form a county for. So rather than a fantasy of returning to a past that was never that glorious, except for a few, or giving up our core freedoms for the fantasy of a future that will never exist, it might be best to finally accept not all Americans want, or will ever want, the same things. This, again, is an example of why the Constitution should be our bedrock.

Most likely the best thing we can ever collectively achieve with our governmental policies is ensuring every citizen as much freedom as possible to find meaning in our own lives. Or as the opening intent from the Declaration of Independence stated, "*We hold these truths to be self-evident, that all men are created equal, that they are endowed by their Creator with certain unalienable Rights, that among these are Life, Liberty and the pursuit of Happiness.*" Individual liberty is the founding concept of America, not any end goal of a homogenous culture all in perfect agreement at all times. America was created with the fundamental goal of ensuring, as much as possible, each and every citizen's freedom from the government and each other. Or as Thomas Jefferson once explained, "*A sound spirit of legislation... banishing all arbitrary and unnecessary restraint on individual action, shall leave us free to do whatever does not violate the equal rights of another.*" In short, this is the concept of popular sovereignty mentioned several times in the book, and a core concept driving our Constitution's creation. Protecting every single person's individual freewill from the government, as well as each other. Ben Franklin said, "*In free governments, the rulers are the servants and the people their superiors and sovereigns.*"

Things can actually come full circle with your "no ideology" ideology when you start to understand and fight for that founding document of our country, the Constitution, and those principles that help it to function the way it was intended. In fact, it could be reasonably argued that the Constitution was written to create the first and closest thing to a "no ideology" government the world has ever known. If the Constitution works, it comes as close as we can get to protecting everyone's right to decide for themselves how to live their own lives, and has no need of political tribes. So, if you are an independent-thinking American, we'd respectfully suggest the Constitution sit atop whatever additional ideals you choose to enhance freedom for all.

Sure, you can vote Republican on one issue, or Democrat on another, but at the end of the day putting every single citizen's right to determine their own lives over any party politics should be the goal. Its what America was created to be, and can still be, with your help. When it comes to politics don't ever be a Republican, or a Democrat, or any other label, before American. That's what a "no ideology" political ideology could be.

Appendix One

Sample Correspondence for Sending to Your Representatives

The letter in this section can be used in its entirety, or selectively cut and pasted to fit your preferred goals. Or, simply use it as a guide to create your own. Once you know what issues and concerns you wish to contact your representatives about, you can spend a few seconds looking up all their contact details on Azavea's free online search at live.cicerodata.com. Most will have email addresses to quickly send them your preferred version of this template. On any of the individual issues, you can even add specific current Congressional bill names of your choice.

Keep in mind, your contact with them does not have to be drawn out or eloquent. In fact, succinct and easy to read is probably better. We'd recommend not stressing about micro-editing the message that much, or even over-thinking your selection of one particular representative over another (heck, send something to them all). Believe it or not, sending almost anything makes a difference as long as it is coherent, because they then get worried knowing you're paying attention. The most important thing is to make some contact regarding the issues that concern you (email, regular post, phone, etc.), and if you really wish to provide pressure on them for positive change, even set a date in the future to follow up with them to make sure they have received your request. Besides for moving toward a more politically independent mindset, and talking to your friends and family about the issues that concern you, this action is probably the easiest to impact change.

(Today's date)

Dear (Congress Woman X, Mayor X, President X, etc),

I am extremely dissatisfied with the current state of American governance. As my representative in it, I would like you to start prioritizing the good of our entire country over your party by addressing the following concerns:

A) Congressional Reform: Congress is currently too partisan, too dysfunctional, and too obsessed with money. I need you to do the following:

1. Create better elections through supporting the Fair Representation Act H.R. 4000, or similar legislation.

2. Make all closed primaries into open primaries by supporting the Open Our Democracy Act from the 115th Congress, or similar legislation.

3. Repeal the 1967 Uniform Congressional District Act and any state-based "sore loser" laws.

4. Support legislation and any other methods to end partisan gerrymandering once-and-for-all.

5. Create, or support, any plans to make the position of Speaker of the House less partisan, including possibly requiring any new speakers to officially renounce party affiliation.

6. Create, or support, efforts to make congressional committees less partisan and more functional, maybe by assigning seats randomly rather than through party loyalty.

7. Reduce, or eliminate, sitting representatives'

fundraising time through legislation similar to Stop Act H.R. 4443 from the 115th Congress.

8. Support any legislation or constitutional amendments that would instill term limits for Congress.

9. Re-create something similar to the Office of Technological Assessment to help keep representatives up to date on rapidly changing technology.

B) Campaign Finance and Ethics Reform: American politics has morally lost its way in regards with money having far too much influence. I need you to do the following:

1. Support American Promise's efforts to enact a Twenty-eighth Amendment to the Constitution for addressing money's role in politics.

2. Support Senator Warren's Anti-Corruption and Integrity Act or similar legislation like Represent Us' American Anti-Corruption Act

C) Presidential Reform. There is an imbalance between constitutional powers, checks and balances, and civil liberties regarding the executive branch, as well as issues regarding how our president is elected. I need you to do the following:

1. Eliminate or reform the Electoral College to better reflect every American's vote carrying equal weight.

2. Eliminate closed presidential primaries.

3. Support ranked-choice voting for President.

4. Reform presidential debate rules to be more inclusive for third parties and independents.

5. Return war powers to constitutional norms through fighting against executive branch abuses of AUMFs and passing legislation to re-establish Congress' need to authorize war.

6. Start or support a bill to require the president to appear before Congress at least twice a year to answer questions and publicly defend his/her policies.

7. Expand presidential rescission powers, and revive the Re-Organization Act to allow the office of president to function more effectively.

8. Correct and prevent any corruption of the office of president through supporting The Presidential Conflict of Interest Act H.R. 371 from the 115th Congress or similar legislation.

D) Supreme Court Reform: The Supreme Court can be less partisan and function better. I need you to do the following:

1. Support enacting term limits on Supreme Court justices.

2. Create or support a constitutional amendment to clearly define what the Supreme Court's mandate should be between an "activist" or "constructionist" role.

E) Additional Reforms and Considerations: There are many other ways you could help the overall function of our government, reduce partisanship, and remove corruption from American politics, like:

1. Fighting to protect the First and Fourth amendments to the Constitution, especially in ways that are increasingly endangered through technological advancements and abuses of laws like The Patriot Act and Freedom Act.

2. Require any state-based overseers of elections, such as secretaries of state, to renounce party affiliation

3. Learn about blockchain technology and its possible beneficial impact on making voting more inclusive and less corrupt, and at least immediately enact laws to protect electronic voting from manipulation and abuse.

4. Consider creating or supporting some sort of agency requirement for media to make efforts at more balanced political coverage, similar to what once existed with the FCC's Fairness Doctrine rule up until 1987, and think about how we can best fight against deepfake technology and social media abuse while still ensuring free speech.

5. Now that you are in office, consider renouncing your own party affiliation, making protection of the US Constitution your main priority, and do the best job you can for the country as a whole rather than any organization or special interest.

Please be advised that I will be observing your actions going forward, and will base my support or opposition of you on them.

Thanks for your time,

(Your Name)
(Your Address)

Again, you can adjust this to emphasize or downplay the issues most important to you, but the important thing is to let them know you're paying attention. Please remember to include your name and mailing address, so that they can be sure you are a voter in their district, and therefore have the ability to withdraw your support if you are displeased with them. Also, if sending an email, it is probably best NOT to include any extra links or attachments, as these will potentially prevent your message from making it through your representative's spam filter.

Appendix Two

Resources for Political Independents

Ideally, we should all be trying to expand our own mind's past the filters of red and blue. Thinking independently and discussing those ideas with your friends and family is actually a hugely impactful way to make grassroots change without much effort. Included below are relatively independent news sources, organizations, books, and resources to help you do this. If you know of, or discover, any others that might be worthy of inclusion in future updates of this book, please feel free to email info@independ.me

***Organizations Attempting to Improve Things That You Might Want to Support*:**
(But always research and come to your own decision)

FairVote.org: Leading the way on congressional election reform to move us toward a more robust democracy.

NoLabels.org: Dedicated to overcoming the right-versus-left polarization of America and finding ways to make government work again through civility, compromise, and accountability.

Independent Voter Network: A central hub of independent news and grassroots movements for people who can no longer stomach being a Republican or Democrat. (ivn.us)

Bridge Alliance: The Bridge Alliance is a unique organization attempting to coordinate the disparate independent and centrist organizations springing up around the country to increase their power and effectiveness. (bridgealliance.us)

Ranked Choice Voting: A group providing coordination and resources for anyone looking to understand and implement RCV in their area. (rankedchoicevoting.org)

Wolf Pac: A little left-leaning, but still overall doing good things on trying to remove money's corruption in politics. (wolf-pac.org)

Equal Citizens: An organization attempting to create electoral reform through strategically targeted state lawsuits. (equalcitizens.us)

Bipartisan Policy Center A Washington-based nonprofit working from within the system to bridge divides between the right and the left, promoting the best ideas of both Republicans and Democrats through compromise and problem-solving. (bipartisanpolicycenter.org)

Open Primaries: This 501c is fighting to banish the practice of the Republicans and Democrats requiring you to join their parties before you can vote. (openprimaries.org)

Fix It America: Another group gaining traction in trying to call an Article V convention to deal with money's corruption of politics. (fixitamerica.org)

Represent Us: An organization dedicated toward abolishing corruption in politics that is organizing periodic "Unrig the System" summits for like-minded independents. (represent.us)

Brennan Center for Justice: Actively working to combat the "rigging" of American democracy, especially in gerrymandering, and a great resource for the status of related legal cases. (brennancenter.org)

First Amendment Coalition: A group fighting to preserve everyone's First Amendment rights, even willing to give you some free legal consultation if you feel like your rights have been violated. (firstamendementcoalition.org)

Open Secrets: A website dedicated to exposing corruption in government and tracking the flow of funds into it. (opensecrets.org)

Move To Amend: Liberal group trying to overturn Citizen's United ruling (movetoamend.org)

Better Angels: A non-profit dedicated toward resolving political polarization in America. (better-angels.org)

Issue One: An cross-partisan organization dedicated to fixing our democracy through increasing governmental ethics and transparency (issueone.org)

Independent Voting: A group dedicated to organizing and supporting independent voters. (independentvoting.org)

The Centrist Project: A group striving to originate many non-two-party solutions, including the "fulcrum strategy" (uniteamerica.org)

Unite America: An organization dedicated to endorsing independent candidates for government in order to break the Republican/Democratic hold. (uniteamerica.org)

American Promise: Organized for the sole purpose of getting a Twenty-eighth Amendment to the Constitution passed for ending the financial corruption of our government. (americanpromise.net)

American Civil Liberties Union: Granted, they often blatantly come down on the political left for many issues, but the ACLU is still the most powerful organization in the country fearlessly fighting to protect civil liberties. (aclu.org)

Partnership for Public Service: A nonpartisan, nonprofit organization dedicated to making government function more efficiently. (ourpublicservice.org)

National Popular Vote: A group getting a lot of momentum on circumventing the worst parts of the Electoral College through an interstate compact. (nationalpopularvote.com)

The Center for Election Science: A group trying to figure out and fight for voting systems that function better and are more inclusive. (electology.org)

New America: Washington think tank trying to bring innovative, nonpartisan solutions into government. (newamerica.org)

Free the People: Libertarian-leaning organization of free-thinkers. (freethepeople.org)

Take Back Our Republic: Group fighting to remove money's corruption of politics (takeback.org)

The Tenth Amendment Center: Los Angeles-based nonprofit fighting to protect the principles of the Tenth Amendment. (tenthamendmentcenter.com)

The Niskanen Center: An independent Washington nonprofit think tank dedicated to creating an "Open Society" defined as: "a social order that is open to political, cultural, and social change; open to free inquiry; open to individual autonomy; open to the poor and marginalized; open to commerce and trade; open to people who may wish to come or go; open to different beliefs and cultures; open to the search for truth; and a government that protects theses freedoms while advancing the cause of open societies around the world." (niskanencenter.org)

Independent Voter Project: Group of nonpartisan activists attempting to enact electoral reform to help independents have a voting voice (independentvoterproject.org)

TermLimits.com: A group gaining great traction on support for imposing congressional term limits once and for all. (termlimits.com)

The Center for Public Impact Interesting group attempting to quantify governmental success, and then use advanced technology like AI to improve it. (thecenterforpublicimpact.org)

Let America Vote Group: A somewhat left-leaning organization attempting to fight against race-based voter suppression tactics throughout the country. (letamericavote.org)

Electronic Frontier Foundation: A group on the forefront of preserving free speech and privacy in digital communication. (eff.org)

FixTheCourts: Group attempting to instill single, eighteen-year term limits for all Supreme Court justices. (fixthecourt.com)

FollowMyVote: Organization attempting to move voting to online blockchain technology so that electoral corruption will be impossible. (followmyvote.org)

Freedom Forum Institute: Nonprofit working to ensure First Amendment rights. (freedomforuminstitute.org)

Institute for Justice: Libertarian law group dedicated to fighting the government for people's rights. (ij.org)

Fourth Amendment Advisory Committee: Organization trying to raise awareness of Fourth Amendment issues and solutions. (fourthadvisory.org)

LegBranch: Nonprofit that describes itself as a transpartisan space to discuss and fight for reforms to Congress to make it function better again. (legbranch.org)

Crossing Party Lines: Group attempting to lessen polarization across the country (crossingpartylines.com)

FreedomWorks: A Libertarian-leaning group with some good resources and grassroots efforts to hold government more accountable (freedomworks.org)

Free the People: A robust libertarian-leaning group trying to expand political conversation past right vs left (freethepeople.org)

Tools to Help You Improve Things

Change.org: A great, simple, free resource for assisting you in creating a viable petition to your government. (Change.org)

Azavea: This group has an amazingly effective, free online tool that you can use to find all of your representatives, from local to state to federal, in a matter of seconds, including all of their contact information. (live.cicerodata.com)

Govtrack.us: An absolutely amazing resource for improving the transparency of government. You can easily find all the bills currently proposed for law, how representatives have voted, and all kinds of other useful information

Votesmart.org: A very cool free resource that allows you to type in any politician's name (even your local reps) to find summaries of their supposed platforms, actual voting records, accepted donations, and even transcripts of past speeches.

Real Clear Politics Congressional Bill Tracker: Similar to VoteSmart, this is an online resource that allows you to search for a particular representative or bill to see summaries, current status, and voting records. (dyn.realclearpolitics.com/congressional_bill_tracker)

Brigade: A very interesting mobile app that will help you create nonpartisan political groups, communicate and enact change, and hold your individual representatives accountable.

Ballotpedia: Sort of an encyclopedia of all things political, this is a useful resource to quickly look up more tedious information regarding current election or legislative stats or facts. (ballotpedia.org)

I Side With: Online quiz you can take that will match your ideologies with candidates and parties... if you trust it to not try and manipulate you (isidewith.com)

Wikileaks: An extremely controversial yet important platform for insiders to disseminate information that powerful groups and people would prefer you to not have. (wikileaks.org)

Constitution Center: A nonpartisan, nonprofit organization raising awareness of the US Constitution, so if you have questions about how the government was actually designed to work, they're a good resource. (constitutioncenter.org)

Protonmail: A free, end to end email encryption provider created by scientists from CERN to send all your subversive communications through (protonmail.com)

National Institute on Money in State Politics: Searchable resource that tracks money's path through governments (followthemoney.org)

PredictIt: Want to find out if someone is going to win reelection, get impeached, pass a law before the event happens, or use the law of large numbers to see some typically accurate predictive odds? Heck, make some money while you're at it. (Predictit.org)

MountVernon: Excellent, easy-to-access free resource of all things George Washington, and much about the other founding fathers and history of revolutionary America. (mountvernon.org)

Signal: A great app for your smart phones that allows you to send secure, encrypted communications (signal.org)

No Labels Policy Recommendations: A thorough report on specific actions the nonpartisan No Labels group recommends for the executive branch. Good to read and discuss with people. (nolabels.org)

United For the People: Website with a lot of great information about current legislation and links to other resources (united4thepeople.org)

National Center for Constitutional Studies Excellent resources for gaining an in-depth understanding of the Constitution and founding of America. (nccs.net)

Bill of Rights Institute: Another excellent source of information and resources on America's history and meaning. (billofrightsinstitute.org)

Cato Institute: If you want a single location to learn about libertarianism, this is probably it (cato.org)

Us Vote Foundation: A one-stop location for keeping your voter registration up to date, as well as finding out polling information for your location. (usvotefoundation.org)

Cook Political Report: Serious analysis and stats of all things political in America (cookpolitical.com)

Independent Sources of News and Information Not Completely Slanted Right or Left

Economist.com: A traditional weekly news magazine out of England, it provides a dense, intellectual and unbiased assessment of America and the world's business and political affairs.

Aljazeera.com As Americans we're trained to get nervous about anything Middle-Eastern sounding, but this is simply a very large news organization which, not being located in America, tends to be much more objective and factual about American politics.

The Anti-Media: Striving to be a hub of independent, nonpartisan news rivaling the propaganda of mainstream media. (theantimedia.com)

Reason.com A true Libertarian opinion (not right-wing extremism) magazine covering the day's big stories with a standard toward objectivity and staying above political propaganda.

Truth Dig: Website attempting to give thoughtful, independent analysis of current topics (truthdig.com)

Vice: Definitely left-leaning but still covering a host of topics largely ignored by mainstream media. (vice.com)

TimCast: Independent reporter Tim Pool's youtube channel often covers topics avoided by the mainstream media (youtube.com TimCast)

We Are Change: YouTube activists trying to find and report the truth, then motivate people to do something about it. (youtube.com WeAreChange)

All Sides: News aggregator geared toward showing news reports from all sides of the political spectrum (allsides.com)

Consortium News: Small organization, but dedicated to independent, investigative journalism in the US. (consortiumnews com)

Truth In Media: A little right-leaning but still making strides to present the facts others aren't talking about. (truthinmedia.com)

Mediaroots.org: Absolutely left-leaning but fearlessly calling out what they see as BS wherever they find it.

Real Clear Politics: RCP doesn't so much refuse to show you anything biased but more tries to provide an aggregate of all the propaganda from all sides on any day's most-pressing political topics, then let's you form your own opinion. (realclearpolitics.com)

The Intercept: Maybe a little left-leaning but dedicated to exposing the truth worldwide, however uncomfortable it is to the powers-that-be. (theintercept.com)

The Guardian: Large news outlet, but not associated with either the US right or left. (theguardian.com)

The Mind Unleashed: Not just covering politics, but a website trying to push boundaries and expand minds (themindunleashed.com)

The Flip Side: A news aggregator giving you multiple sources of news from the right, left, and center each day. (theflipside.io)

Podcasts and Shows Worth Listening to or Watching:

Congressional Dish: Amazingly dedicated host Jen Briney reads—yes, actually reads—all the bills being considered for becoming law by each Congress so you don't have to, then lets you know all the bullshit, shenanigans, and overall disgusting "sausage-making" going on in relation to each. (congressionaldish.com)

Common Sense: Easily one of the most independent and insightful analysts of current political developments, Dan Carlin has been cutting through partisan bullshit for years... when he's not on break from his shows, that is. (dancarlin.com)

Independent Voter Network Podcast: Just like it sounds, a podcast dedicated to informing you of the potential nonpartisan solutions to pressing issues of the day. (ivn.us/podcasts)

CitizenFour: Excellent documentary showing Edward Snowden's efforts to expose mass illegal governmental surveillance by the US in real-time. (amazonprime or itunes)

Lions of Liberty: Yes, it is obviously highlighting Libertarian Party principles, but also delves into the related ideas of political reform, reducing corruption, and holding our dysfunctional government more accountable. (lionsofliberty com)

American Swamp: MSNBC 2019 mini-series about dark money influence in our politics (msnbc.com)

Decode DC: A former Washington staffer turned lobbyist turned reformer lets you know how things work behind the scenes. (decodedc.com)

The Corbett Report A long-running podcast with a unique open-source intelligence gathering system that often provides facts the mainstream media would rather you not know. (corbettreport.com)

Left, Right, and Center: KCRW attempts to get a liberal, a conservative, and a centrist in a room together each week to debate current political headlines. Good for broadening your perspective on how different people think. (kcrw com)

The Joe Rogan Experience: Easily one of the deepest yet funniest podcasts available. Rogan doesn't often directly cover politics, but you can rest assured whoever he has on his show will be unique, and their discussion will involve fascinating concepts. Just pick a guest you think might be interesting and go. (podcasts.joerogan.net)

Hacking Democracy: Now over ten years old, this documentary about how hackable and potentially corrupt our voting systems are around the country was terrifying when it originally came out, but might be even more so now, as so little has been done in that time to address the problems. (hackingdemocracy.com)

The Deadly Isms: A seven part libertarian-leaning mini-series that explores the dangers of many historical political movements. (available on Amazon Prime)

The Politics Guys: Three guys with backgrounds in political science bringing independent analysis to all things government. (politicsguys.com)

The Freedom Report: One-time Senatorial contender Austin Petersen gives a Libertarian analysis of the day's issues.

(thelibertarianrepublic.podbean.com)

The Weeds: A deep dive into current political topics. (vox.com/the-weeds)

Hip Hughes History: If you need a quick, entertaining video brush up on any number of different historical concerns, including but not limited to politics, go here. (youtube.com/hughesDV)

Another Way Podcast: Relatively new but created by the extremely knowledgeable Professor Lawrence Lessig, this is sure to offer some brilliant ideas for improving the function of our government. (equalcitizens.us/anotherway)

Tom Woods Show: Unapologetically Libertarian, Woods is still an Ivy-League-educated scholar worth listening to for innovative ideas outside the mainstream. (tomwoods.com)

My History Can Beat Up Your Politics: Historian tries to elevate analysis of current political topics by taking a look at the reality of America's past. (myhistorycanbeatupyourpolitics.wordpress.com)

Crash Course US Government: Excellent series of short, free videos from PBS that explain how US government works.

Third Parties Maybe Worth Checking Out
(But Entirely up to You if You Support or Not)

Serve America Movement: SAM values and goals appear very closely align with this book. It apparently does not try to get members to agree on every facet of political ideology, but is focusing on ending corruption by the two-party system and enhancing democracy for all. (joinsam.org)

United Independent Party: Despite the immediate catch-22 of independents all joining together in a group, and the inherent weirdness and fanaticism that seems to often develop in any political party no matter how good its founding intentions, their principles at least seem to be starting off on the right track. (uiparty.org)

Libertarian Party: In its core principles, Libertarianism is pretty great in advocating smaller government and greater personal freedom for everyone. In reality there's been some right-wing nut jobs hiding behind the Libertarian banner in recent years, but as the most viable third party in the country currently, it probably worth fighting for. (lp.org)

Modern Whig Party: Another newer party formed on centrist ideas and hoping to appeal to those that are sick of the extremism of both the Republicans and Democrats. (modernwhig.org)

Reform Party: Past their brief national heyday in the 1990s, the Reform Party can still sometimes make an impact on state and local elections, while also attempting to cater to a largely centrist message. (reformparty.org)

The Green Party: Very left-leaning on many issues but raises some good points and tends to have a strong following in certain parts of the country. (gp.org)

Constitution Party (constitutionparty.com) Promoting itself as fighting for "integrity, liberty and prosperity," they appear to be making some inroads on various state's ballots

Books to Consider Reading for Deeper Independent Thinking

Republic, Lost by Lawrence Lessig: If you're looking for the most thorough examination of how money corrupts our government, and why it is so tricky to fix, start here.

Constitution 3.0, Freedom and Technological Change by Jeffrey Rosen: Jeffrey Rosen is a knowledgeable authority clearly explaining and warning against the systemic dangers of recent technological changes to our constitutional rights—and what to do about it.

A Declaration of Independents by Greg Orman: A politician's take on how to break from from two-party control.

American Gospel by Jon Meachem: An extremely objective and fascinating study of what the founding fathers actually thought about God and religions.

The Three Languages of Politics by Arnold King: An interesting look at how social paradigms and language in the US guide people into bracketed thinking regarding politics.

This Town by Mark Leibovich: A fascinating journalistic glance into the slimy social workings of the world's most powerfully corrupt city by a reporter who has lived in the trenches.

The Case Against the Supreme Court by Erwin Chemerinsky: A somewhat "progressive" take on the failures of the Supreme Court throughout American history, but worthwhile to think about what the court's role should ideally be.

A Short History of Progress by Ronald Wright: Interesting take on the ways "progress" inevitably comes with unforeseen errors, disasters, and challenges.

The Politically Incorrect Guide to the US Constitution by Kevin Gutzman: Granted, there are many justifiable interpretations of the meaning and best-use principles of the Constitution with no single person or group having sacrosanct knowledge, but this Libertarian-leaning analysis provides some important and often overlooked interpretations in our modern debates.

Democracy Incorporated by Sheldon S. Wolin: Insightful look into the explosion of corporate lobbying influence on politics through recent decades.

The Voting Wars by Richard Hansen: Good book for an overall understanding of how both parties are corrupting individual elections, and how precarious the situation could become in the future.

Reclaiming the American Revolution by William J Watkins: A good argument about how our government is actually supposed to work based on the Kentucky and Virginia resolutions.

Plutocrats United by Richard Hansen: A balanced and insightful look at the modern state of money's corruption of politics.

Two Tribes: Unique, illustrated children's book apparently geared towards helping kids learn how to get past the binary thinking of adult's caught in right vs left (twotribesbook.com)

A People's History of the United States by Howard Zinn: A history of the United States from the perspective of the nameless groups of people bearing the brunt of government and businesses decisions rather than the more recognized individuals at the top making them.

The Politically Incorrect Guide to American History by Tom Woods: A unique and often-overlooked perspective on American history from Libertarian Tom Woods.

The Age of Surveillance Capitalism by Shoshana Zuboff: A detailed look into the inherent threats to society from an upcoming age of digital surveillance.

Solutions to Political Polarization in America by Nathaniel Persily: A book of essays from various political analysts (some left-leaning, some right-leaning) proposing solutions to our modern polarization. Worth reading, if only to realize where you don't agree with some "expert" opinions.

American Sovereigns by Christian Fritz: An extremely detailed look at the concept of popular sovereignty through American history.

The Parties Versus the People by Mikey Edwards: An excellent book from a former Congressman giving concrete suggestions of how to fix Washington from the inside out.

The New Confessions of an Economic Hitman by John Perkins: Although there is dispute over the validity of some of his assertions and reasoning, the book can still help you analyze US foreign policy and unbridled capitalism through a new lens.

American Nations by Colin Woodard: A unique perspective on the cultural history of America, helping to explain its current regional and economic divisions

And last, this book will be periodically updated to keep information current and relevant.

Please go to **independ.me** to sign up for our newsletter. Our goal is to help facilitate an ongoing nexus for independent political movements and thinkers. It would also help if you subscribed to the **"Independ Me" youtube channel**. Also, if you have any suggestions for future additions or subtractions for the book, please feel free to email us through **info@independ.me**

Appendix Three

Notes on the Current Congress
(the 116th as of this book edition)

Ideally, this book would be able to tell you exactly what bills and what politicians to support at any given time. Logistically however, that is impossible, even if we knew all the right answers (which we probably don't), as there are simply too many variables and moving parts in the making of American laws to keep even a website flawlessly current at all times, let alone something that is actually put into print.

To help illustrate the difficulties, consider that at the time this book was going to print almost 7500 bills had already been proposed in the two-year long 116th Congress, even though it was not yet half way done. Looking back through recent history, it is safe to assume there will easily be well over 10,000 potential laws suggested before the 116th congressional session comes to an end in 2020. Many of these bills overlap in their scope and goals, are made up of dozens or hundreds of pages, and often contain conflicting or troublesome earmarks, amendments, and partisan objectives, even if they ostensibly fight for something good on the surface. Prior to making it all the way through both houses of Congress any bill can even change by various committee dealings, so what you thought was a good idea to begin with turns into something altogether unacceptable by the time it is signed into law.

If you'd like a refresher on how a bill becomes a law, we'd suggest you go to GovTrack.us to watch a couple of quick videos. Suffice to say, it is a messy business, therefore, please take any suggestions of specific legislation to support as just that, a suggestion at a particular moment in time.

The best that can really be done with this book is for you to understand the principles you are fighting for, and then look for possible laws and candidates to support that with the least amount of shenanigans attached. Being in its very nature incomplete, we will still attempt to provide a current (within each Congress) non-partisan reference list of proposed bills and representatives who, on at least some level, are appearing to make an effort to support some independent ideals. As each two year Congressional session comes to an end, however, all of the un-passed laws, and possibly even some of the representatives, will disappear. That's why understanding the principle you are fighting for, rather than just a bill or person's name, is crucial to continuing the fight for change going forward.

Again, a few things to keep in mind:

- This list is not exhaustive, and will change as bills, politicians, and Congress' change.

- By listing a bill or politician, it is not a whole-hearted endorsement of every position and action they take, only stating they may be worth your extra consideration of support for that issue. Just because a Republican or Democrat is possibly doing something good on one issue, does not mean the entire party or platform on other issues is correct. And it is okay to support a politician's efforts on one issue, and disagree with them on others.

- The bills and candidates listed should primarily be used as references for yourself, and maybe as examples in your communication with your representatives and associates about changes you wish to make. If you understand the issue and the bill does not get passed this Congress, you can fight to get it re-introduced in the next.

- Remember these are all politicians, so they often lie. For all we know these bills could actually just end up being laws to enslave us, or turn us into human beef stew, but... occasionally you just have to go for it.

Electoral Reform Solutions

Rep Donald Beyer D-VA
HR 4000 The Fair Representation Act

Rep Grace Meng D-NY
HR 394 21st Century Voting Act

Rep Zoe Lofgren D-CA
HR 2722 SAFE Act

Open Primaries Solutions

Senator John Delaney D-MD
HR 2981 115th Open Our Democracy Act

Rep Brian Fitzpatrick R-PA
HR 163 CLEAN Elections Act

Gerrymandering Solutions

Rep Jerry McNerney D-CA
HR 2057 Fair Map Act

Senator Michael Bennet D-CO
S 1972 Fair Maps Act

Rep Zoe Lofgren D-CA
HR 3572 Redistricting Reform Act

Senator Amy Klobuchar D-MN
S 2226 A Bill To Require Independent Redistricting

Rep Sheila Jackson Lee D-TX
HR 44 Coretta Scott King Mid-Decade Redistricting Prohibition Act

Term Limits Solutions

Senator Ted Cruz R-TX
SJ Res 1 Constitutional Amendment for Congressional Term Limits

Rep Brian Fitzpatrick R-PA
HJ Res 12 Constitutional Amendment to Impose Term Limits on Congress

Rep Ralph Norman R-SC
HR 198 The VOICE Act

Rep Trey Hollingsworth R-IN
HJ Res 14 Term Limit Amendment

Electoral College Solutions

Rep Steve Cohen D-TN
HJ Res 7 Constitutional Amendment to Abolish the Electoral College

Senator Brian Schatz D-HI
SJ Res 17 Constitutional Amendment to Abolish the Electoral College

Senator Jeff Merkley D-OR
SJ Res 16 Constitutional Amendment to Abolish the Electoral College

Financial Reform and Ethics Solutions

Derek Kilmer D-WA
HR 1272 Restoring Integrity to America's Elections Act

Rep Theodore Deutch D-FL
HR 812 Conflicts from Political Fundraising Act

Rep Kathleen Rice D-NY

HR 679 Political Accountability and Transparency Act

Rep Susan Davis D-CA
HR 137 Federal Election Integrity Act

Senator Elizabeth Warren D-MA
S 882 Presidential Conflict of Interest Act

Rep Ted Lieu D-CA
HR 706 Restoring Public Trust Act

Senator Ron Wyden D-CA
S 20 Presidential Tax Transparency Act

Rep Alma Adams D-CA
HR 2332 TRUST Act

Rep Kathleen Clark D-MA
HR 1481 Presidential Accountability Act

Senator Tom Udall D-NM
S 51 Democracy for All Amendment

Rep Stephen Lynch D-MA
HR 391 White House Transparency Act

Rep Jamie Raskin D-MD
HR 745 Executive Branch Comprehensive Ethics Enforcement Act

War Powers Solutions

Rep James Himes D-CT
HR 1193 Reclamation of War Powers Act

Rep Peter DeFazio D-OR
HJ Res 66 War Powers Amendments Act

More Politicians Possibly Thinking Independently

Rep Justin Amash R-MI
For publicly leaving the two-party system

Rep Tulsi Gabbard D-HI
For her efforts to fight for Constitutional norms

Senator Rand Paul R-KY
For his efforts to fight for Constitutional norms

Appendix Four

The United States Constitution

We the People of the United States, in Order to form a more perfect Union, establish Justice, insure domestic Tranquility, provide for the common defence, promote the general Welfare, and secure the Blessings of Liberty to ourselves and our Posterity, do ordain and establish this Constitution for the United States of America.

Article. I.

Section. 1.

All legislative Powers herein granted shall be vested in a Congress of the United States, which shall consist of a Senate and House of Representatives.

Section. 2.

The House of Representatives shall be composed of Members chosen every second Year by the People of the several States, and the Electors in each State shall have the Qualifications requisite for Electors of the most numerous Branch of the State Legislature.

No Person shall be a Representative who shall not have attained to the Age of twenty five Years, and been seven Years a Citizen of the United States, and who shall not, when elected, be an Inhabitant of that State in which he shall be chosen.

Representatives and direct Taxes shall be apportioned among the several States which may be included within this Union, according to their respective Numbers, which shall be determined by adding to the whole Number of free Persons, including those bound to Service for a Term of Years, and excluding Indians not taxed, three fifths of all other Persons. The actual Enumeration shall be made within three Years after the first Meeting of the Congress of the United States, and within every subsequent Term of ten Years, in such Manner as they shall by Law direct. The Number of Representatives shall not exceed one for every thirty Thousand, but each State shall have at Least one Representative; and until such enumeration shall be made, the State of New Hampshire shall be entitled to chuse three, Massachusetts eight, Rhode-Island and Providence Plantations one, Connecticut five, New-York six, New Jersey four, Pennsylvania eight, Delaware one, Maryland six, Virginia ten, North Carolina five, South Carolina five, and Georgia three.

When vacancies happen in the Representation from any State, the Executive Authority thereof shall issue Writs of Election to fill such Vacancies.
The House of Representatives shall chuse their Speaker and other Officers; and shall have the sole Power of Impeachment.

Section. 3.

The Senate of the United States shall be composed of two Senators from each State, chosen by the Legislature thereof, for six Years; and each Senator shall have one Vote.
Immediately after they shall be assembled in Consequence of the first Election, they shall be divided as equally as may be into three Classes. The Seats of the Senators of the first Class shall be vacated at the Expiration of the second Year, of the second Class at the Expiration of the fourth Year, and of the third Class at the Expiration of the sixth Year, so that one third may be chosen every second Year; and if Vacancies happen by Resignation, or otherwise, during the Recess of the Legislature

of any State, the Executive thereof may make temporary Appointments until the next Meeting of the Legislature, which shall then fill such Vacancies.

No Person shall be a Senator who shall not have attained to the Age of thirty Years, and been nine Years a Citizen of the United States, and who shall not, when elected, be an Inhabitant of that State for which he shall be chosen.

The Vice President of the United States shall be President of the Senate, but shall have no Vote, unless they be equally divided.

The Senate shall chuse their other Officers, and also a President pro tempore, in the Absence of the Vice President, or when he shall exercise the Office of President of the United States.

The Senate shall have the sole Power to try all Impeachments. When sitting for that Purpose, they shall be on Oath or Affirmation. When the President of the United States is tried, the Chief Justice shall preside: And no Person shall be convicted without the Concurrence of two thirds of the Members present.

Judgment in Cases of Impeachment shall not extend further than to removal from Office, and disqualification to hold and enjoy any Office of honor, Trust or Profit under the United States: but the Party convicted shall nevertheless be liable and subject to Indictment, Trial, Judgment and Punishment, according to Law.

Section. 4.

The Times, Places and Manner of holding Elections for Senators and Representatives, shall be prescribed in each State by the Legislature thereof; but the Congress may at any time by

Law make or alter such Regulations, except as to the Places of chusing Senators.

The Congress shall assemble at least once in every Year, and such Meeting shall be on the first Monday in December, unless they shall by Law appoint a different Day.

Section. 5.

Each House shall be the Judge of the Elections, Returns and Qualifications of its own Members, and a Majority of each shall constitute a Quorum to do Business; but a smaller Number may adjourn from day to day, and may be authorized to compel the Attendance of absent Members, in such Manner, and under such Penalties as each House may provide.

Each House may determine the Rules of its Proceedings, punish its Members for disorderly Behaviour, and, with the Concurrence of two thirds, expel a Member.
Each House shall keep a Journal of its Proceedings, and from time to time publish the same, excepting such Parts as may in their Judgment require Secrecy; and the Yeas and Nays of the Members of either House on any question shall, at the Desire of one fifth of those Present, be entered on the Journal.

Neither House, during the Session of Congress, shall, without the Consent of the other, adjourn for more than three days, nor to any other Place than that in which the two Houses shall be sitting.

Section. 6.

The Senators and Representatives shall receive a Compensation for their Services, to be ascertained by Law, and paid out of the Treasury of the United States. They shall in all Cases, except Treason, Felony and Breach of the Peace, be privileged from

Arrest during their Attendance at the Session of their respective Houses, and in going to and returning from the same; and for any Speech or Debate in either House, they shall not be questioned in any other Place.

No Senator or Representative shall, during the Time for which he was elected, be appointed to any civil Office under the Authority of the United States, which shall have been created, or the Emoluments whereof shall have been encreased during such time; and no Person holding any Office under the United States, shall be a Member of either House during his Continuance in Office.

Section. 7.

All Bills for raising Revenue shall originate in the House of Representatives; but the Senate may propose or concur with Amendments as on other Bills.
Every Bill which shall have passed the House of Representatives and the Senate, shall, before it become a Law, be presented to the President of the United States; If he approve he shall sign it, but if not he shall return it, with his Objections to that House in which it shall have originated, who shall enter the Objections at large on their Journal, and proceed to reconsider it. If after such Reconsideration two thirds of that House shall agree to pass the Bill, it shall be sent, together with the Objections, to the other House, by which it shall likewise be reconsidered, and if approved by two thirds of that House, it shall become a Law. But in all such Cases the Votes of both Houses shall be determined by yeas and Nays, and the Names of the Persons voting for and against the Bill shall be entered on the Journal of each House respectively. If any Bill shall not be returned by the President within ten Days (Sundays excepted) after it shall have been presented to him, the Same shall be a Law, in like Manner as if he had signed it,

unless the Congress by their Adjournment prevent its Return, in which Case it shall not be a Law.

Every Order, Resolution, or Vote to which the Concurrence of the Senate and House of Representatives may be necessary (except on a question of Adjournment) shall be presented to the President of the United States; and before the Same shall take Effect, shall be approved by him, or being disapproved by him, shall be repassed by two thirds of the Senate and House of Representatives, according to the Rules and Limitations prescribed in the Case of a Bill.

Section. 8.

The Congress shall have Power To lay and collect Taxes, Duties, Imposts and Excises, to pay the Debts and provide for the common Defence and general Welfare of the United States; but all Duties, Imposts and Excises shall be uniform throughout the United States;

To borrow Money on the credit of the United States;

To regulate Commerce with foreign Nations, and among the several States, and with the Indian Tribes;

To establish an uniform Rule of Naturalization, and uniform Laws on the subject of Bankruptcies throughout the United States;

To coin Money, regulate the Value thereof, and of foreign Coin, and fix the Standard of Weights and Measures;

To provide for the Punishment of counterfeiting the Securities and current Coin of the United States;

To establish Post Offices and post Roads;

To promote the Progress of Science and useful Arts, by securing for limited Times to Authors and Inventors the exclusive Right to their respective Writings and Discoveries;

To constitute Tribunals inferior to the supreme Court;

To define and punish Piracies and Felonies committed on the high Seas, and Offences against the Law of Nations;

To declare War, grant Letters of Marque and Reprisal, and make Rules concerning Captures on Land and Water;

To raise and support Armies, but no Appropriation of Money to that Use shall be for a longer Term than two Years;

To provide and maintain a Navy;

To make Rules for the Government and Regulation of the land and naval Forces;

To provide for calling forth the Militia to execute the Laws of the Union, suppress Insurrections and repel Invasions;

To provide for organizing, arming, and disciplining, the Militia, and for governing such Part of them as may be employed in the Service of the United States, reserving to the States respectively, the Appointment of the Officers, and the Authority of training the Militia according to the discipline prescribed by Congress;

To exercise exclusive Legislation in all Cases whatsoever, over such District (not exceeding ten Miles square) as may, by Cession of particular States, and the Acceptance of Congress, become the Seat of the Government of the United States, and to exercise like Authority over all Places purchased by the Consent of the Legislature of the State in which the Same shall be, for the Erection of Forts, Magazines, Arsenals, dock-Yards, and other needful Buildings;—And

To make all Laws which shall be necessary and proper for carrying into Execution the foregoing Powers, and all other Powers vested by this Constitution in the Government of the United States, or in any Department or Officer thereof.

Section. 9.

The Migration or Importation of such Persons as any of the States now existing shall think proper to admit, shall not be prohibited by the Congress prior to the Year one thousand eight hundred and eight, but a Tax or duty may be imposed on such Importation, not exceeding ten dollars for each Person.

The Privilege of the Writ of Habeas Corpus shall not be suspended, unless when in Cases of Rebellion or Invasion the public Safety may require it.

No Bill of Attainder or ex post facto Law shall be passed.

No Capitation, or other direct, Tax shall be laid, unless in Proportion to the Census or enumeration herein before directed to be taken.

No Tax or Duty shall be laid on Articles exported from any State.

No Preference shall be given by any Regulation of Commerce or Revenue to the Ports of one State over those of another: nor shall Vessels bound to, or from, one State, be obliged to enter, clear, or pay Duties in another.

No Money shall be drawn from the Treasury, but in Consequence of Appropriations made by Law; and a regular Statement and Account of the Receipts and Expenditures of all public Money shall be published from time to time.

No Title of Nobility shall be granted by the United States: And no Person holding any Office of Profit or Trust under them, shall, without the Consent of the Congress, accept of any

present, Emolument, Office, or Title, of any kind whatever, from any King, Prince, or foreign State.
Section. 10.
No State shall enter into any Treaty, Alliance, or Confederation; grant Letters of Marque and Reprisal; coin Money; emit Bills of Credit; make any Thing but gold and silver Coin a Tender in Payment of Debts; pass any Bill of Attainder, ex post facto Law, or Law impairing the Obligation of Contracts, or grant any Title of Nobility.
No State shall, without the Consent of the Congress, lay any Imposts or Duties on Imports or Exports, except what may be absolutely necessary for executing it's inspection Laws: and the net Produce of all Duties and Imposts, laid by any State on Imports or Exports, shall be for the Use of the Treasury of the United States; and all such Laws shall be subject to the Revision and Controul of the Congress.
No State shall, without the Consent of Congress, lay any Duty of Tonnage, keep Troops, or Ships of War in time of Peace, enter into any Agreement or Compact with another State, or with a foreign Power, or engage in War, unless actually invaded, or in such imminent Danger as will not admit of delay.

Article. II.

Section. 1.

The executive Power shall be vested in a President of the United States of America. He shall hold his Office during the Term of four Years, and, together with the Vice President, chosen for the same Term, be elected, as follows
Each State shall appoint, in such Manner as the Legislature thereof may direct, a Number of Electors, equal to the whole Number of Senators and Representatives to which the State may be entitled in the Congress: but no Senator or Representative, or Person holding an Office of Trust or Profit under the United States, shall be appointed an Elector.

The Electors shall meet in their respective States, and vote by Ballot for two Persons, of whom one at least shall not be an Inhabitant of the same State with themselves. And they shall make a List of all the Persons voted for, and of the Number of Votes for each; which List they shall sign and certify, and transmit sealed to the Seat of the Government of the United States, directed to the President of the Senate. The President of the Senate shall, in the Presence of the Senate and House of Representatives, open all the Certificates, and the Votes shall then be counted. The Person having the greatest Number of Votes shall be the President, if such Number be a Majority of the whole Number of Electors appointed; and if there be more than one who have such Majority, and have an equal Number of Votes, then the House of Representatives shall immediately chuse by Ballot one of them for President; and if no Person have a Majority, then from the five highest on the List the said House shall in like Manner chuse the President. But in chusing the President, the Votes shall be taken by States, the Representation from each State having one Vote; A quorum for this Purpose shall consist of a Member or Members from two thirds of the States, and a Majority of all the States shall be necessary to a Choice. In every Case, after the Choice of the President, the Person having the greatest Number of Votes of the Electors shall be the Vice President. But if there should remain two or more who have equal Votes, the Senate shall chuse from them by Ballot the Vice President.

The Congress may determine the Time of chusing the Electors, and the Day on which they shall give their Votes; which Day shall be the same throughout the United States.
No Person except a natural born Citizen, or a Citizen of the United States, at the time of the Adoption of this Constitution, shall be eligible to the Office of President; neither shall any Person be eligible to that Office who shall not have attained to

the Age of thirty five Years, and been fourteen Years a Resident within the United States.

In Case of the Removal of the President from Office, or of his Death, Resignation, or Inability to discharge the Powers and Duties of the said Office, the Same shall devolve on the Vice President, and the Congress may by Law provide for the Case of Removal, Death, Resignation or Inability, both of the President and Vice President, declaring what Officer shall then act as President, and such Officer shall act accordingly, until the Disability be removed, or a President shall be elected.

The President shall, at stated Times, receive for his Services, a Compensation, which shall neither be encreased nor diminished during the Period for which he shall have been elected, and he shall not receive within that Period any other Emolument from the United States, or any of them.

Before he enter on the Execution of his Office, he shall take the following Oath or Affirmation:—"I do solemnly swear (or affirm) that I will faithfully execute the Office of President of the United States, and will to the best of my Ability, preserve, protect and defend the Constitution of the United States."

Section. 2.

The President shall be Commander in Chief of the Army and Navy of the United States, and of the Militia of the several States, when called into the actual Service of the United States; he may require the Opinion, in writing, of the principal Officer in each of the executive Departments, upon any Subject relating to the Duties of their respective Offices, and he shall have Power to grant Reprieves and Pardons for Offences against the United States, except in Cases of Impeachment.

He shall have Power, by and with the Advice and Consent of the Senate, to make Treaties, provided two thirds of the Senators present concur; and he shall nominate, and by and with the Advice and Consent of the Senate, shall appoint Ambassadors, other public Ministers and Consuls, Judges of the supreme Court, and all other Officers of the United States, whose Appointments are not herein otherwise provided for, and which shall be established by Law: but the Congress may by Law vest the Appointment of such inferior Officers, as they think proper, in the President alone, in the Courts of Law, or in the Heads of Departments.

The President shall have Power to fill up all Vacancies that may happen during the Recess of the Senate, by granting Commissions which shall expire at the End of their next Session.

Section. 3.

He shall from time to time give to the Congress Information of the State of the Union, and recommend to their Consideration such Measures as he shall judge necessary and expedient; he may, on extraordinary Occasions, convene both Houses, or either of them, and in Case of Disagreement between them, with Respect to the Time of Adjournment, he may adjourn them to such Time as he shall think proper; he shall receive Ambassadors and other public Ministers; he shall take Care that the Laws be faithfully executed, and shall Commission all the Officers of the United States.

Section. 4.

The President, Vice President and all civil Officers of the United States, shall be removed from Office on Impeachment for, and Conviction of, Treason, Bribery, or other high Crimes and Misdemeanors.

Article III.

Section. 1.

The judicial Power of the United States, shall be vested in one supreme Court, and in such inferior Courts as the Congress may from time to time ordain and establish. The Judges, both of the supreme and inferior Courts, shall hold their Offices during good Behaviour, and shall, at stated Times, receive for their Services, a Compensation, which shall not be diminished during their Continuance in Office.

Section. 2.

The judicial Power shall extend to all Cases, in Law and Equity, arising under this Constitution, the Laws of the United States, and Treaties made, or which shall be made, under their Authority;—to all Cases affecting Ambassadors, other public Ministers and Consuls;—to all Cases of admiralty and maritime Jurisdiction;—to Controversies to which the United States shall be a Party;—to Controversies between two or more States;—between a State and Citizens of another State,—between Citizens of different States,—between Citizens of the same State claiming Lands under Grants of different States, and between a State, or the Citizens thereof, and foreign States, Citizens or Subjects.
In all Cases affecting Ambassadors, other public Ministers and Consuls, and those in which a State shall be Party, the supreme Court shall have original Jurisdiction. In all the other Cases before mentioned, the supreme Court shall have appellate Jurisdiction, both as to Law and Fact, with such Exceptions, and under such Regulations as the Congress shall make.

The Trial of all Crimes, except in Cases of Impeachment, shall be by Jury; and such Trial shall be held in the State where the said Crimes shall have been committed; but when not committed within any State, the Trial shall be at such Place or Places as the Congress may by Law have directed.

Section. 3.

Treason against the United States, shall consist only in levying War against them, or in adhering to their Enemies, giving them Aid and Comfort. No Person shall be convicted of Treason unless on the Testimony of two Witnesses to the same overt Act, or on Confession in open Court.

The Congress shall have Power to declare the Punishment of Treason, but no Attainder of Treason shall work Corruption of Blood, or Forfeiture except during the Life of the Person attainted.

Article. IV.

Section. 1.

Full Faith and Credit shall be given in each State to the public Acts, Records, and judicial Proceedings of every other State. And the Congress may by general Laws prescribe the Manner in which such Acts, Records and Proceedings shall be proved, and the Effect thereof.

Section. 2.

The Citizens of each State shall be entitled to all Privileges and Immunities of Citizens in the several States.

A Person charged in any State with Treason, Felony, or other Crime, who shall flee from Justice, and be found in another State, shall on Demand of the executive Authority of the State from which he fled, be delivered up, to be removed to the State having Jurisdiction of the Crime.

No Person held to Service or Labour in one State, under the Laws thereof, escaping into another, shall, in Consequence of any Law or Regulation therein, be discharged from such Service or Labour, but shall be delivered up on Claim of the Party to whom such Service or Labour may be due.

Section. 3.

New States may be admitted by the Congress into this Union; but no new State shall be formed or erected within the Jurisdiction of any other State; nor any State be formed by the Junction of two or more States, or Parts of States, without the Consent of the Legislatures of the States concerned as well as of the Congress.
The Congress shall have Power to dispose of and make all needful Rules and Regulations respecting the Territory or other Property belonging to the United States; and nothing in this Constitution shall be so construed as to Prejudice any Claims of the United States, or of any particular State.

Section. 4.

The United States shall guarantee to every State in this Union a Republican Form of Government, and shall protect each of them against Invasion; and on Application of the Legislature, or of the Executive (when the Legislature cannot be convened), against domestic Violence.

Article. V.

The Congress, whenever two thirds of both Houses shall deem it necessary, shall propose Amendments to this Constitution, or, on the Application of the Legislatures of two thirds of the several States, shall call a Convention for proposing Amendments, which, in either Case, shall be valid to all Intents and Purposes, as Part of this Constitution, when ratified by the Legislatures of three fourths of the several States, or by Conventions in three fourths thereof, as the one or the other Mode of Ratification may be proposed by the Congress; Provided that no Amendment which may be made prior to the Year One thousand eight hundred and eight shall in any Manner affect the first and fourth Clauses in the Ninth Section of the first Article; and that no State, without its Consent, shall be deprived of its equal Suffrage in the Senate.

Article. VI.

All Debts contracted and Engagements entered into, before the Adoption of this Constitution, shall be as valid against the United States under this Constitution, as under the Confederation.

This Constitution, and the Laws of the United States which shall be made in Pursuance thereof; and all Treaties made, or which shall be made, under the Authority of the United States, shall be the supreme Law of the Land; and the Judges in every State shall be bound thereby, any Thing in the Constitution or Laws of any State to the Contrary notwithstanding.

The Senators and Representatives before mentioned, and the Members of the several State Legislatures, and all executive and judicial Officers, both of the United States and of the several States, shall be bound by Oath or Affirmation, to support this Constitution; but no religious Test shall ever be required as a Qualification to any Office or public Trust under the United States.

Article. VII.

The Ratification of the Conventions of nine States, shall be sufficient for the Establishment of this Constitution between the States so ratifying the Same.

The Word, "the," being interlined between the seventh and eighth Lines of the first Page, The Word "Thirty" being partly written on an Erazure in the fifteenth Line of the first Page, The Words "is tried" being interlined between the thirty second and thirty third Lines of the first Page and the Word "the" being interlined between the forty third and forty fourth Lines of the second Page.

Attest William Jackson Secretary

done in Convention by the Unanimous Consent of the States present the Seventeenth Day of September in the Year of our Lord one thousand seven hundred and Eighty seven and of the Independance of the United States of America the Twelfth In witness whereof We have hereunto subscribed our Names,

Chapter References

Chapter 1 References

Noonan, Peggy, *Rage is Rage*, Wall Street Journal, June 15th, 2017

Pew Research Center, *Political Polarization 1994-2107*, October 2017

Inequality.org

Bernstein, Lenny, *US Life Expectancy Fall Again*, Washington Post, November 29th, 2018

Chalabi, Mona, *How Bad is US Gun Violence?*, The Guardian, October 5th, 2017

Levine, Steve; Canipe, Chris, *40% in U.S. Can't Afford Middle-Class Basics*, Axios, May 16th, 2018

Peter G Petersen Foundation, *CBO Report Highlights Unsustainable Fiscal Outlook*, Feb 1st, 2019

The Economist, *Declining Trust in Government is Denting Democracy*, January 25th, 2017

Hedges, Chris, *The Coming Collapse*, TruthDig, May 20th, 2018

Chapter 2 References

Psychology Encyclopedia, psychology.jrank.org

Gehl, Katherine M.; Porter, Michael E., *Why Competition in the Politics Industry is Failing America*, Harvard Business School, 2017

Freakanomics Radio, Episode 356, *America's Hidden Duopoly*, October 31st, 2018

Gilens, Martin; Page, Benjamin I., *Testing Theories of American Politics*, Princeton University, 2014 represent.us, Unbreaking America, 2019

Lessig, Lawrence, *Republic Lost*, Hachette Book Group, October 5th, 2011

Chapter 3 References

Domenico, Montanaro, 2 *Party System? Americans Might be Ready for 8*, NPR.org, October 24th, 2017

Schmitt, Mark, *Why America Should Have More Than 2 Political Parties*, Vox, September 16th, 2016

Chapter 4 References

FairVote.org, *Monopoly Politics,* Updated yearly since 1997

Edwards, Mickey, *The Parties Versus the People*, Yale University Press, 2012

Davenport, David, *A Growing Cancer on Congress: The Curse of Party-Line Voting*, Forbes, December 13th, 2017

FairVote.org, *Fair Representation*

Miller, Paul David, *How to Burn Down the Two-Party System*, The Federalist, June 1st, 2016

ballotpedia.org, Ranked-Choice-Voting

Dean, Howard, *How to Move Beyond the Two-Party System*, The New York Times, October 7th, 2016

Fair Representation Act (HR3057), FairVote.org, introduced to Congress in June of 2017

represent.us, American Anti-Corruption Act

azavea.com

Ballotpedia.org

change.org

Gehl, Katherine M.; Porter, Michael E., *Why Competition in the Politics Industry is Failing America*, Harvard Business School, 2017

Dickerson, Brian, *How Partisan Primaries Weaken the Political Center*, Detroit Free Press, November 15th, 2017

openprimaries.org

Open Our Democracy Act (HR2981), John Delaney

openourdemocracy.com

Independent Voter's Network

Colbenz, Michael, *The Two Party System is Destroying America*, The Hill, January 28th, 2016

Kang, Michael S., *Sore Loser Laws and Democratic Contestation*, Emory University, 2011

Ingraham, Christopher, *This is the Best Explanation of Gerrymandering You Will Ever See*, Washington Post, March 1st, 2015

Payne-Riley, Lauren, *Solutions to Gerrymandering*, policymap.com, August 7th, 2017

The Brennan Center for Justice, *Redistricting*

Stephanopoulus, Nick; McGhee, Eric, *Partisan Gerrymandering and the Efficiency Gap*, University of Chicago, 2014

nolables.org, *The Speaker Project*

60 Minutes, *Dialing for Dollars*, CBS, April 24th, 2016

Jolly, David, *Stop Act (HR4443)*, 115th Congress, 2015

UniteAmerica.org, *Fulcrum Strategy*

NoLabels.org , *Problem Solvers Caucus*

termlimits.com

Chapter 5 References

Black, Eric, *10 Reasons Why the Electoral College is a Problem*, MinnPost, October 16th, 2012

nationalpopularvote.com

Boxer, Barbara, Joint Resolution 41

equalcitizens.us

azavea.com

wikipedia.org, Graduated Random Presidential Primary System

openprimaries.org

Delaney, John, *Open Our Democracy (HR2981)*

fairvote.org, American Plan

represent.us, American Anti-Corruption Act

change.org

Raeburn, Paul, *How Election 2016 Would Be Different With Ranked Choice Voting*, Newsweek, October 17th, 2016

Zollman, Kevin, Carnegie Mellon University

Orman, Greg, *Why Ranked Choice Voting Makes Sense*, Real Clear Politics, October 16th, 2016

fairvote.org, ranked choice voting

rankedchoicevoting.org

electology.org

changetherule.org

Cruz, Melissa, *Third Parties See Chance for Spot in Presidential Debates*, Real Clear Politics, February 10th, 2017

University of Pennsylvania's Annenberg Public Policy Center

Briney, Jen, *Congressional Dish*, Episode 117

Rand, Paul, nolables.org, *Policy Playbook*, 2016

Warren, Elizabeth, *Presidential Conflicts of Interest Act* (HR371), 116th Congress

Brennan Center For Justice, National Task Force on Rule of Law and Democracy

Chapter 6 References

Kreig, Gregory, *Our Flimsy Campaign Finance and Lobbying Laws*, CNN, May 14th 2018

opensecrets.org

wikipedia.org

Lessig, Lawrence, *Republic Lost*, Hachette Book Group, October 5th, 2011

Hughes, Keith, *Citizens United Explained*, Hip Hughes History, Youtube, April 12th, 2013

americanpromise.net

represent.us

Meyer Alexander, Raquel Meyer; Mazza, Stephen W; & Scholz, Susan, *Measuring Rates of Return for Lobbying Expenditures,* University of Kansas, 2004

Briney, Jen, *Intro to Lobbying*, Congressional Dish, Ep100

Williams, Jimmy, *I Was a Lobbyist for More Than Six Years*, Vox, January 5th, 2018

Drutman, Lee, How Corporate *Lobbyists Conquered American Democracy*, The Atlantic, April 20th, 2015

Warren, Elizabeth, *Anti-Corruption and Integrity Act*

Martin, Abby

Chapter 7 References

Perry, Barbara A, *Original Intent or Evolving Constitution?*, American Bar Association, 2004

fixthecourt.com

tenthamendementcenter.com

Gutzman, Kevin, *The Politically Incorrect Guide to the Constitution*, Regnery Publishing, 2007

Woods, Thomas E, *The Politically Incorrect Guide to American History*, Regnery Publishing Group, 2004

Watkins, William J, *Reclaiming the American Revolution*, Palgrave MacMillan, 2004

American Legislative Council

Daniels, Gilda R, *Outsourcing Democracy*, University of Baltimore, 2011

Hansen, Rick, *The Voting Wars*, Talking Points Memo, August 20th, 2012

Chapter 8 References

Rottman, Gabe, *Free Speech for Some Means Free Speech for None*, ACLU, October 22th, 2014

firstamendmentcoalition.org

freedomforuminstitute.org

aclu.org

Poitraus, Laura, *CitizenFour*, Praxis Films, 2014

Briney, Jen, *Congressional Dish*, Episode 98

Bischoff, Paul, *A Breakdown of the Patriot Act, Freedom Act, and FISA*, Comparitech, 2018

Balko, Radley, *Surprise! Controversial Patriot Act Power Now Used Overwhelmingly in Drug Investigations*, Washington Post, October 29th, 2018

Rosen, Jeffrey, *Jeffrey Rosen on the Fourth Amendment and Privacy*, constitutioncenter.org

eff.org

fourthadvisory.org

nacdl.org

aclu.org

ij.org

Guynn, Jessica, *California Passes Nation's Toughest Online Privacy Law*, USA Today, June 28th, 2018

Chapter 9 References

Spoonamore, Stephen, ABC News, June 2012

DEFCON 26, PBS News, August 12th, 2018

Teale-Edwards Productions, *Hacking Democracy,* hackingdemocracy.com, HBO, 2006

Institute for the Future, *Understand How Block-Chain Works in Under Two Minutes*, Youtube, April 12th, 2016

followmyvote.com

verifiedvoting.com

Butler, Josh, *How America Can Benefits from Australia's Compulsory Voting System*, Huffpost, March 6th, 2018

Carter, Stephen, *Want More Voters? Pay Them*, Bloomberg, April 2nd, 2015

nitrd.gov

centerforpublicimpact.org

e-estonia.com

Tibken, Shara, *Questions to Mark Zuckerberg Show Many Senators Don't Get Facebook*, Cnet, April 8th, 2018

Burgat, Casey; Kosar, Kevin, *OK, So the House Wants to Reform Itself? Here's What It Should Really Do*, Politico, January 29th, 2019

legbranch.org

Lessig, Lawrence, *Republic Lost*, Hachette Book Group, October 5th, 2011

Gehl, Katherine M.; Porter, Michael E., *Why Competition in the Politics Industry is Failing America*, Harvard Business School, 2017

Cole, Samantha, *This AI-Generated Joe Rogan Voice Sounds So Real It's Scary*, Vice, May 17th, 2019

How Finland is Winning the War Against Fake News, CNN, May 17th, 2019

ballotpedia.org / ballot initiative

ncls.org

Made in the USA
Middletown, DE
22 September 2020

20375055R00154